Do It Yourself
HR BASICS
FOR SMALL BUSINESS

Write Your Own HR Policies

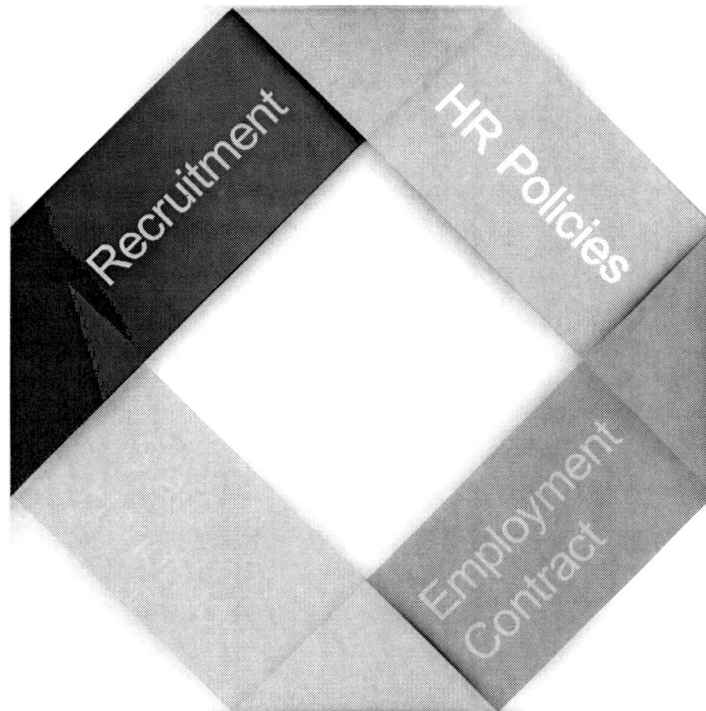

Recruitment

HR Policies

Employment Contract

JulieKelly HR
SUPPORTING SMALLER BUSINESSES

DO IT YOURSELF HR FOR SMALL BUSINESS

Volume 1

Write Your Own HR Policies

Julie Kelly

ONION CUSTARD PUBLISHING LTD

Do it Yourself HR for Small Business
Write Your Own HR Policies

The information provided in this book is designed to provide helpful information and guidance to writing your own Human Resources policies within current UK guidelines. The information provided is accurate at the time of going to print (Second Edition, July 2014). The Publisher and Author are not responsible for any errors caused by changes in legislation after the publication date, or for any misinterpretation of the content on the part of the user. If you have any doubt about your competence in using these policies for your business it is strongly advised that you seek competent professional advice.

References are provided for informational purposes only and do not constitute endorsement of any websites or other sources. No contract is implied in the use of the informaiton in this book between the user and either the Publisher, or the Author. Readers should be aware that the websites listed in this book may change.

Published in the United Kingdom by Onion Custard, Cardiff, UK.
http://publishing.onioncustard.com

Paperback format: ISBN: 978-1-909129-63-4

First Edition: November, 2013
Second Edition: July 2014
Third Edition: September 2014

Category: Personnel & Human Resources Management

Contents

Introduction

Human Resources (HR), Employment Legislation, Policies and Procedures, Contracts of Employment... topics that most small business owners try to avoid. This is generally because of a feeling of being out of their depth. There's so much to think about, so many laws and regulations... so where to start?

Rather than start at all, many small business owners opt instead to ignore HR issues, hoping they will go away. That is fine, until you have a problem, then there's nothing to fall back on – no guidelines, no procedures, no idea of what your rights are, or those of your employee(s).

As a small business owner myself, I know how important it is to watch the pennies, I also know that demands on cashflow are high. However, employment legislation does not make allowances for the individual circumstances of your business, and, whether you like it or not, if you employ staff you are expected to provide them with a safe and secure place of work. At the very least you must provide them with the minimum adequate protection as advised under various legal statutes. This book has arisen from a demand from the small business owners I meet for an affordable, manageable means to achieving comprehensive HR management.

You don't need any experience or knowledge to use this book. It provides you with easy to follow guidelines on writing the essential policies your business to protect both you and your staff. It is the first in a set of do it yourself human resources tools, designed to effectively and economically manage the HR function of your business. It's often the last thing entrepreneurs consider, yet human resources – your people – are such a key element to the success of your business.

By the end of this book you will have a set of six HR policies and procedures, ready to put in place at your business.

This book is suitable for all small businesses. It provides all the material you need to write full and adequate policies. It is not intended for larger organisations that have their own human resources facility.

Why do I Need all these Policies and Procedures?

If you are either new to employment, or already employ staff but do not have any policies and procedures in place, it is often tempting to obtain a policy for the sake of saying you have one. Just to look good. However, a policy should be more than just words on paper, it should be relevant and easy to follow. This book will provide both you and your staff with guidelines and consistency, and prevent problems caused by misunderstandings and poor staff morale.

I hear a lot of comments about why HR isn't important, or even relevant to the business owner. It generally starts with, "I don't really need HR because..."

- My business is too small to need Human Resources
- It doesn't apply in my line of work
- I don't have the time
- HR is just politically-correct mumbo jumbo
- I don't understand it
- There's too much to know
- I don't employ anyone, they are all self-employed
- I only employ temps
- I can't afford to employ an HR person
- I work the old-fashioned way. If they don't listen I show them the door

Let's tackle some of these questions to see how they hold up in the eyes of the law, and how they might affect your bottom line.

"My business is too small to need Human Resources."

If you employ just one member of staff you are obligated by law to provide them with a contract of employment and put in place a range of policies.

"It doesn't apply in my line of work."

HR applies in every line of work, there are no exemptions in the world of business.

"I don't have the time."

Good HR should save you time. Yes, if you go down this route it will take time initially but, once in place, it will make the day-to-day running of your business easier, more efficient and more profitable. Good HR can positively affect your bottom line.

"HR is just politically-correct mumbo jumbo."

Unfortunately the high profile cases that hit the news tend to feature topical stories that are surrounded by bureaucracy. 'Ivory Tower' HR, as I call it, can be very directive and full of 'best practice' solutions that once filtered down do not always work. Personally I favour processes that are tailored to your company needs and keep things simple and easy to follow. Good HR is always a benefit to both employer and employee.

"I don't understand it."

HR can be complicated, and the constant changes to legislation don't help. The policies in this book are written in easy to understand terms, and whereas legislation needs to be adhered to, and referred to, the ones you'll find here are written in a procedural way so they can be followed. That means they enhance your company, rather than detract from it. You don't have to know everything about HR. Chances are, you don't know everything about every aspect of your business, so you hire people to do those things better. That's why you have staff in the first place. This book can help you complete your first, basic HR Policies – if you need to understand more – ask a specialist.

"There's too much to know."

The purpose of a good policy is so that you don't need to know everything, but the answers are there to refer to as and when required. For example, you may not need to know right now the ins and outs of maternity legislation, but should an employee come to you in three months' time and advise you that she is pregnant then you first pull out your policy and refer to the relevant section. That's when any additional research can come in. Complete these templates and you have a basic framework which sets out what you need to do, should the event arise.

"I don't employ anyone, they are all self-employed."

Even if all your employees are self employed or contractors, if they are working for you, or at your place of work, you need to ensure there are adequate policies in place to protect them and/or guide them. You have duties and obligations that extend beyond the people you directly employ. If you work with freelancers on an regular basis, you might want to include them in your policies. After all, if they are that valuable to your business you might want to offer incentives to hang on to them.

"I only employ temps."

As with self employed staff, you need to ensure your workplace is running smoothly, and is compliant with legislation.

"I can't afford to emply an HR person."

HR *can* be an expensive option, but it doesn't *have* to be. Indeed, by following this book you can reduce your costs even further, without jeopordising the quality of your policies. Rather than getting an HR specialist to draft everything from scratch, you can present them with these templates already completed. They only need to make minor changes, and you come to the exercise with considerably more knowledge than you would otherwise.

"I don't need HR, I only employ friends and family."

This is probably one of the most common reasons I hear from small business owners. Unfortunately, this is one of the main causes of dispute. It is true that we feel more comfortable trusting friends and family with our livelihood, and this is great until there is a difference of opinion that could forever lose that friendship and trust. Even when you employ a friend or family member, if you have a contract of employment and policies in place there is no confusion and both parties know where they stand.

> **FACT: if you employ staff, they *automatically* gain rights and protection under the *Employment Rights Act 1996*.**

Ignoring HR will not make your obligations simply go away. You don't choose to opt-in to this, it's the law. And here's the thing, HR can actually be good for your business! It's not all about having to do the bare minimum to comply with the law. You can actually use these tools to build a happier, more motivated workforce. That means fewer sick days, better productivity, and longer retention of staff.

Who are These Templates Suitable For?

These templates are suitable for small business owners who are:

- Self-employed
- Partnerships
- Limited companies
- Charitable and not for profit organisations
- Retail outlets
- Any business that employs at least one member of staff

This book provides you with the basic policies you will require, explained in easy to understand language. It will enable you to have policies and procedures quickly in place that are relevant to your company, and not just a file of paper gathering dust somewhere. If you operate good policies your company will grow faster and become more productive. If you increase the quality of your staff morale, and ensure their wellbeing, you might expect to see a rise in their productivity and that means improved profits.

The policies in this book compliment the other titles in the *Do It Yourself HR Basics* series, and you can find more details of these at the end of this book. Polices are just one aspect of the management of the people in your business. It takes a little work, but investing in your workforce may be the best use of your time and money. These DIY guides are a reduced version of the full product that I offer my clients which includes one to one consultation and is called *HR Basics for Small Businesses*.

How to Use These Templates

I have divided the book into six sections, each relating to one type of policy. Each section provides all the information you will need to draw up that policy and establish a simple, clear, and comprehensive procedure.

1: Disciplinary Policy Template

2: Absence & Sickness Policy Template

3: Annual Leave Policy Template

4: Grievance Policy Template

5: Maternity/Paternity/Adoption Policy Template

6: Equality Policy Template

Each section is accompanied by explanations of the implications of including, or omitting, clauses and their relevance.

> **The comments you see written like this are for your information. You should obviously not include these comments in your policy!**

To make it really obvious I have underlined all of the content that is a legal requirement (in the style of this paragraph). Taking these parts out won't mean you can ignore them, they will still apply under the law. They should remain underlined in your Policy wording, with a note that they are a legal requirement, for the benefit of your staff and managers alike. You need to be aware at all times what your minimum legal obligations are.

You will see this box at the top of each section:

> *Your Company Name:*
>
> *Referred to in this policy as "The Company"*

This allows you to simply copy the content in the section without having to replace text with your company name every time. You can, if you chose to, remove this.

It's worth noting, however, that you may be required to change some wording – where you see (date) or (named person), for example. These policies are designed to be do-it-yourself, just ensure that you read each policy wording carefully and make any customisations as required by your own business needs. However, I'd urge you not to re-write sections, merely omit the ones you don't need. The policy wordings here are accurate and legal – you need to be careful when wording things yourself as it's all too easy to use inappropriate, ambiguous, misleading, or just plain wrong words.

Can I Trust This Content?

Absolutely. The contents of this book are from a trusted, relaible and regularly updated HR industry source. As a result, you can be sure that the content is accurate date at the time of publication, and reflects the latest changes in Government Policy, HR guideines and best practice.

I have been an HR professional for over 25 years, and use the same source on a daily basis when I provide custom solutions for small businesses just like yours. It's my job to stay on top of changes, and to advise clients on where they may need to make changes, or when new laws create major new challenges to their business. Whether you use my services or not on an ongoing basis, I really want to impress on you the need for regular review and improvement of your HR policies and processes.

Your HR policies have to be working documents, the law changes and your business will need to follow suit. Don't treat these policies as write-and-forget, review them at least annually and check with regulation changes to ensure you continue to comply. Remember the adage, "Ignorance of the law is no excuse." You can't shrug your shoulders in a couple of years time and claim you didn't know a particular change affected your business, the Judge won't see it that way.

This exercise should be the start of your HR process, rather than being merely a paper exercise to satisfy others. When HR is done well, and policies and procedures are well thought through, it leads to better run businesses, with fewer employee disputes. Everyone knows where they stand, and that provides clarity and clear leadership.

So, on with the policies, and I wish you well in producing your own set of legal, far and robust HR Policy and Procedures.

How do I Customise The Templates Without Having to Re-Type Them?

You can receive a blank MS Word version of these policy documents by contacting my Publisher, Onion Custard Publishing, at hrpolicies@onioncustard.com. You will need to verify your purchase by sending a copy of your purchase receipt, and then you can get your templates, ready to customise. They should, of course, be used in conjunction with this book as they don't contain the notes and comments.

Alternatively, if you require some advice and guidance on your specific circumstances, you can purchase the full version of *HR Basics for Small Businesses* or HR Basics for charities at www.juliekellyhr.co.uk, or you can contact me for bespoke advice by emailing julie@juliekellyhr.co.uk. The initial consultation is free of charge and without obligation, and the majority of my work is conducted on a fixed-fee basis that is agreed in advance.

1: Disciplinary Policy & Procedure

We all like to think that we will never have to use this policy but, unfortunately, when you employ people there is always a chance that you will need to take disciplinary action. It is important that you have a Disciplinary Policy and Procedure in place, as it provides you, your managers, and your staff, with clear and structured guidelines.

The Disciplinary Policy that follows is very comprehensive. It takes into account all governing legislation and, if followed correctly, it will ensure your company keeps within the law. It deals with disciplinary matters quickly and fairly.

A Disciplinary Policy should always begin with an introduction setting out the responsibilities of all the parties that are likely to be involved in applying it. It should then be followed by a short paragraph outlining who the procedure applies to. Another short paragraph on its aims, i.e. *why* the policy and procedure is necessary.

Below are the core principles of the policy. It is essential that they are followed. Where it refers to an investigation, this could simply consist of meetings between the parties involved, or in more serious investigations it may require the input of an experienced HR professional. If in doubt – seek advice. There is general advice available from organisations such as *ACAS* or you can contact an HR consultant (such as myself!). Note though that the investigation meeting is not in itself a disciplinary meeting. You always need to carry out your formal disciplinary meeting as set out in the procedures.

Disciplinary action, no matter how small or trivial it may seem, must be carried out in a timely manner, and in line with procedure, otherwise you open yourself up for further problems. There's already a serious issue to deal with, don't compound it with bad practices.

The flexibility of missing a stage is outlined below to enable you to conclude a disciplinary after a verbal warning, if the situation is resolved or minor. On the other hand, if it is a serious issue, then you also have the flexibility to go straight to the final stages of the process.

If you feel it is necessary to suspend someone whilst you are carrying out your investigation you need to ensure you have good reasons for doing this and also that you make it very clear that no blame or predetermined decision has been made.

Disciplinary meetings should always be structured and pre-arranged. It is advisable that you ask an employee that is not involved in the matter (one you can be sure will respect and adhere to the confidentially of the situation) to act as a witness and note-taker. If you do not have such an employee you may ask an external witness.

The employee(s) involved in the disciplinary also have the right to be accompanied, as outlined in your policy. It is your responsibility to advise the employee of this in advance, and to ensure they are aware that the person accompanying them must not prejudice the hearing in any way. They are there to support the employee and they are allowed to speak on behalf of the employee. However; any questions asked directly to the employee must only be answered by them.

Always invite the employee to the disciplinary in writing. This may seem unnecessary in a small organisation but it is very important. It is also important to give them sufficient warning, and to create an auditable paper trail. You may need to demonstrate in the future that you followed due process, and a paper trail is how you'll achieve this.

At the start of the meeting the person chairing it should outline the format and explain the process.

You may only record the meeting if ALL parties present agree in advance (video or audio).

If necessary, adjourn the meeting, but bear in mind that this should only be done if there is a real need. These meetings are never pleasant and the quicker they are over with the better for everyone involved.

Once you have all the information, go through it and make informed decisions. Document your decisions and reasons so you can refer back to them, particulary in cases where is it possible that it could end in a dismissal. Bear in mind that the first, apparently trivial disciplinary matter *could* be the first of many, so document them all in the same way and you are covered in the future. Ensure that the process is carried out by a person in a senior position (and/or an HR consultant) with sufficient experience of carrying out investigations.

In cases where a decision is made that will impact on other people, or will have on-going consequences, ensure all actions are documented in writing and all parties sign to say they have read and understand them. It is important in such cases that future actions are carried out. If there is a deadline placed on any action (e.g. if an employee is told that they have six months to improve) a review meeting should be scheduled, and if satisfactory results achieved (or no further incidents occur) then the action should be removed.

Always advise employees of their right to appeal in line with this process.

Disciplinary Policy & Procedure

Introduction

In any organisation there is a need for rules and standards. It is important that any breaches of our rules, or failure to achieve and maintain satisfactory standards of conduct, attendance and job performance, are dealt with effectively, fairly and consistently.

This procedure is non-contractual, and sets out the procedure The Company will normally follow, although we reserve the right, at our discretion, to vary, replace or terminate the procedure at any stage.

All managers are reminded of the requirement to comply with the ACAS Code of Practice on Disciplinary and Grievance Procedures.

Scope of this procedure

This procedure applies to all employees, other than those in their probationary period.

Aims of this procedure

This procedure aims to help and encourage all of our employees to achieve and maintain satisfactory standards and to ensure consistent and fair treatment for all.

Core principles

The following core principles should be followed by those dealing with disciplinary matters:

General

- *No disciplinary action will be taken without full and proper investigation.*

- *In misconduct cases, where practicable, different people will carry out the investigation and disciplinary hearings. An investigatory meeting will not by itself result in any disciplinary action.*

- *Each step in the procedure will be taken without unreasonable delay, the timing and location of any meetings will be reasonable and any meeting will be held in as private a location as possible without interruptions.*

- *A fair disciplinary process will always be followed, up to and including cases of dismissal for gross misconduct.*

- *We may omit any of the stages within the disciplinary procedure detailed below. It should be noted that, despite ongoing disciplinary action, an individual may be dismissed for another unrelated disciplinary matter if sufficiently serious.*

Suspension

Except for paid suspension (used purely as a precautionary measure to allow a fair and impartial investigation to take place, and without any prejudgement of the outcome of any subsequent disciplinary hearing), no action will be taken against an employee until a disciplinary hearing has been held.

Invitation to hearing

The employee will always be given written notice of an invitation to any disciplinary hearing of which he or she is the subject, and will be advised of the nature of the complaint against him/her, the circumstances that have led to us contemplating the need for disciplinary action or dismissal and the procedure to be followed. Copies of any written evidence will normally be provided in advance of the hearing.

The employee will be given sufficient information and time to enable him/her to prepare a response. This may vary depending on the circumstances of each case but is not likely to be less than 24 hours.

If either the employee or his/her chosen companion is unable to attend any meeting under this procedure for a reason that was not foreseeable at the time the meeting was arranged, then we will attempt to rearrange the meeting for a date within five working days of the original planned date. However, the employee is expected to take all reasonable steps to attend the hearing on the appointed date and at the appointed time. Where an employee persistently is unable or unwilling to attend an agreed disciplinary meeting, without good reason, a decision may be made in the employee's absence based on the evidence available.

At the hearing

*At all formal stages of this procedure, the person chairing the meeting is advised to be accompanied by a suitable employee of **The Company** who will act as a witness and take full notes of everything that is said. Where no internal person of sufficient seniority or confidential status is available, or where preferred, an external party may be invited to attend in this capacity.*

Under no circumstances should any meeting or conversation be recorded without the prior permission of those present.

In addition, the employee will have the right to be accompanied, either by a fellow worker, a representative of a trade union (who must be certified in writing by that union as having experience of, or having received training in, acting as a worker's companion at disciplinary or grievance hearings) or an official employed by a trade union. The employee should tell the person conducting the hearing in advance whom he or she has requested to act as a companion. It would not normally be reasonable for an employee to insist on being accompanied by someone whose presence would prejudice the hearing nor would it be reasonable to ask to be accompanied by someone from a remote geographical site if someone suitable and willing is available on site.

The companion is there to act as a witness to what was said, to provide moral support and to assist and advise the employee in presenting his/her case. He or she may address the hearing (provided the employee wishes this), ask questions on behalf of the employee and confer with the employee but not answer questions on behalf of the employee. Nor may the companion prevent the employer from explaining its case. <u>Fellow workers may not be compelled to attend as a companion.</u>

<u>If the employee is disabled, reasonable adjustments will be made to ensure that he or she is not disadvantaged at the hearing.</u> This may include the provision of further assistance (eg for a signer or other support) where necessary. Arrangements may also be made to assist any employee who does not have English as his or her first language and who may need an interpreter.

<u>The person conducting the disciplinary hearing will explain the complaint against the employee and go through the evidence that has been gathered. The employee will be given the opportunity to present any information in his/her defence, explain or comment before any decision is made. Either party may ask questions, call witnesses, submit witness statements and also question any witnesses called by the other party.</u> If the employee wishes to call any witnesses, he or she should notify the person conducting the hearing in advance. <u>Witnesses cannot be compelled to attend.</u>

A disciplinary hearing may be adjourned at any stage by the person conducting the hearing, in order to calm a tense situation, to check out facts or to take advice. Such adjournments will be kept brief wherever possible in order not to hold up the resolution of the hearing but may be extended where particular information needs to be checked in the interests of fairness or consistency.

Making a decision

Before making any decision on disciplinary action, we will take into account the employee's disciplinary and general record, any similar precedents, any mitigating circumstances or explanations given by the employee, what would be reasonable under the circumstances and whether any training, additional support or adjustments to the role or workload are necessary.

An employee who is given a disciplinary warning or improvement note will be told where his/her performance or conduct falls short of what we consider satisfactory, what improvement in conduct or performance is required, and over what timescale this is to be achieved. For employees who are under-performing, a review date will be set and we will also confirm any support, including any training that we will provide to assist the employee.

<u>A decision to dismiss should only be taken by someone with the authority to do so. The reasons for dismissal will be confirmed in writing, together with the date on which the employment will end, the appropriate period of notice and the right of appeal.</u>

Post hearing

<u>Any warning or improvement note will be confirmed in writing to the employee. It will outline what the next stage in the procedure is (should the employee fail to reach a satisfactory standard or commit a further act of misconduct), specify for how long it will stand, and will inform the employee of his or her right of appeal.</u>

If the employee's standard of work or conduct remains unsatisfactory, and, after warnings, remains below the level that is acceptable, he/she may be dismissed.

It is important that your employees know what behaviours or actions are serious enough to warrant being classed as either gross or general misconduct. The lists included in this policy are fairly comprehensive, but you may decide on further industry-specific examples, or indeed you may decide that some of them are not relevant to you and remove them. This is OK, it's *your* policy and needs to work for *your* business.

Examples of gross misconduct

The list below is not exhaustive but is a guide to the type of offence which normally results in summary dismissal (i.e. dismissal without notice or pay in lieu of notice):

- *theft, fraud or falsification of records e.g.company documentation, expense claims or attendance records etc*

- *being under the influence of alcohol*

- *being in possession of, or under the influence of, non-medically prescribed drugs*

- *assault or fighting, either on our premises or whilst engaged on our business or where the act committed irrevocably damages the required trust and mutual confidence between the company and the employee*

- *violent, abusive or intimidating conduct*

- *act of unlawful discrimination, harassment, bullying or offensive behaviour*

- *misuse of property belonging to the company or of our name*

- *malicious damage to property belonging to the company, our clients/customers or other employees*

- *flagrant disregard of our procedures, rules and regulations*

- *any action in serious breach of legislative requirements which may affect our business*

- *gross negligence*

- *use of foul language or any act that violates commonly accepted standards of behaviour*

- *actions which damage the reputation of the company or bring it into disrepute - this includes taking part in activities which result in adverse publicity to ourselves, or which cause us to lose faith in your integrity*

- *any action constituting a criminal offence which makes you unsuitable for employment with us*

- *unauthorised use or disclosure of confidential information*

- *failure to disclose correct information on your application form*

- *serious breach of Health and Safety rules*

- *accepting a gift which could be construed as a bribe*

- *acts of dishonesty*

- *undertaking private work on our premises and/or during working hours without express permission*

- *accepting gifts from outside organisations which have not been approved by **The Company***

- *smoking in an unauthorised area where this constitutes a serious risk to health and safety or compromises our products*

- *driving whilst under the influence of unlawful drugs or alcohol*

- *sleeping on duty*

- *inappropriate use of the Internet or computer misuse in breach of our policies. This includes deliberately accessing sites containing pornographic, offensive or obscene material.*

- *Using a hand held mobile device whilst driving on in control of a company vehicle at any time, or whilst driving or in control of large or dangerous equipment.*

An employee will not normally be dismissed for a first incident of misconduct, unless it amounts to gross misconduct, in which case summary dismissal without notice and without the need for any prior warnings may take place.

Examples of general misconduct

The following is a non-exhaustive list of examples of offences, which amount to misconduct falling short of gross misconduct:

- *unauthorised absence from work*

- *unsatisfactory time-keeping or attendance*

- *unsatisfactory job performance*

- *time wasting*

- *failure to follow a reasonable management instruction*

- *minor contravention of health and safety regulations*

- *disruptive behaviour*

- *unauthorised use of the telephone*

- *unauthorised use of e-mail and/or the internet*

- *failure to wear personal protective equipment, if issued*

- *minor damage to our property*

- *minor breach of our rules*

- *leaving your place of work without authority*

- *failing to notify us of your absence from work*

- *persistent absence/sickness*

- *taking extended breaks*

- *disrupting our business by receiving and making what we consider to be excessive personal telephone calls.*

Informal counselling

You may think that counselling suggests costly fees: this need not be the case. Counselling is often best sought from fellow employees who understand the situation, and what is required to enable the employee to improve. A good example of this is a mentor, or one of the employees' peers. Whichever route you decide, always ensure you action it in writing.

We recognise that cases of minor misconduct or poor performance may best be resolved through informal counselling, goal or target setting, advice or training and these do not form a formal part of this procedure.

Where an improvement is required, we will ensure that the employee understands what is required, how this will be measured, and over what period. Any agreed action plan will be confirmed in writing.

Where a sustained improvement is not apparent, or where matters are more serious or where the issue is one of misconduct, the formal disciplinary procedure will be used.

Stages of the procedure

I cannot emphasise enough the importance of following procedure when conducting any type of investigative meeting, and a disciplinary meeting is no exception. Ensuring your policy/procedure is structured with easy to follow sections makes what is sometimes a very difficult situation easier to handle. A disciplinary procedure needs to outline the various stages, even though it may not always be necessary to visit each stage. It is not necessary to list every tiny possibility, but a brief explanation of what each stage represents will provide more guidance and structure to all involved and mitigate misunderstandings.

1. *Verbal warning for unsatisfactory performance or misconduct of a relatively minor nature*

2. *First written warning (or improvement note) for incidents of misconduct or unsatisfactory performance*

3. *Final written warning for further continued unsatisfactory performance or further misconduct or if an incident of serious misconduct occurs*

4. *Dismissal with notice for continued unsatisfactory performance or conduct.*

Gross misconduct and summary dismissal

Certain offences may be regarded as so serious as to render the employee liable to summary dismissal without prior warning (see examples above). A dismissal for gross misconduct will only be made following a disciplinary hearing and will be confirmed in writing, giving the reasons for dismissal, confirming that the employment terminates immediately without notice, or pay in lieu of notice, and outlining the employee's right of appeal.

Penalties other than dismissal

There may be circumstances where we consider alternative disciplinary action to dismissal to be appropriate. Such action could include suspension without pay, demotion (which may result in a reduction in pay for the employee), or transfer to another position, which may result in a reduction of pay.

14

Suspension

We reserve the right at any stage of this procedure to suspend the employee. Suspension will be on full basic pay and will be for as short a period as possible in order to carry out any investigation of an alleged serious offence or to prevent any recurrence. Such suspension is not disciplinary action and does not involve any prejudgement.

If suspended, the employee must be available to attend any fact-finding interview called during the suspension period. Contact will be maintained with the employee throughout the period of suspension to keep him/her informed of the investigation. An employee who is suspended will only be allowed to contact the company through a nominated person.

Only a Director of the company is permitted to authorise suspension.

Appeal

Regardless of the stage the process is at, an employee must be given the right to appeal the decision. A clear appeals procedure will help all parties, and ensure consistency and fairness. An appeal should never be seen as paying lip service, and should always be treated impartially.

An employee who feels that a disciplinary warning, improvement note, or dismissal is unfair may appeal against this. Such appeals should be lodged, in writing, without unreasonable delay (we would expect this to be within seven calendar days of the decision being notified to the employee).

The employee should clearly state the grounds on which the appeal is made (e.g. the finding is unfair, the penalty too harsh, new evidence comes to light, or because of a procedural defect).

An appeal hearing will be arranged without unreasonable delay. Where possible, the appeal will normally be heard by a member of staff senior to the person making the original decision and not previously connected with the disciplinary process so that an independent decision may be made. If this is not possible, a further independent party or other external party may be requested to attend the hearing and advise.

The person conducting the appeal is advised to be accompanied by a suitable employee of the company who will act as a witness and take full notes of everything that is said. Where no internal person of sufficient seniority or confidential status is available, or where preferred, an external party may be invited to attend in this capacity.

The employee may, if he/she so wishes, be accompanied by a work colleague, a trade union representative (who must be certified in writing by that union as having experience of, or having received training in, acting as a worker's companion at disciplinary or grievance hearings) or by an official employed by a trade union at any appeal hearing.

The employee should tell the person conducting the appeal hearing in advance whom he or she has chosen as a companion. As with a disciplinary hearing, the companion will be able to address the hearing, ask questions on behalf of the employee and to confer with the employee but not to answer questions on behalf of the employee.

If either the employee or his/her chosen companion is unable to attend an appeal meeting arranged under this procedure for a reason which was not foreseeable at the time the meeting was arranged, we will attempt to rearrange the meeting for a date within five days of the original planned date.

If the employee is disabled, reasonable adjustments will be made to ensure that he or she is not disadvantaged at the hearing. This may include the provision of further assistance where necessary.

Arrangements may also be made to assist any employee who does not have English as his or her first language and who may need an interpreter.

The grounds of the appeal will be considered when deciding the extent of any new investigation: it may be that a complete re-hearing will be held should there be any suspected procedural defects.

The employee will be notified of the appeal decision in writing: whatever decision is taken at the appeal hearing will be final.

2: Absence & SicknessPolicy

Absence is one of the major issues faced by small businesses. A major illness or stress-related condition can have a devastating affect on both the running of the business, and the morale of other staff. It is essential to get your absence and sickness policy in place. It may not *stop* the absence but it will enable you to *control* it.

> *Your Company Name:*
>
> *Referred to in this policy as "The Company"*

Introduction

We are sympathetic to genuine cases of illness or other problems which might make absence unavoidable. However, excessive or unauthorised absence causes disruption to the business and lowers the morale of other staff. Therefore, all absences are taken seriously and unnecessary absence is likely to lead to disciplinary action.

This policy is not contractual but sets out the way in which The Company plans to deal with absence at work.

Scope of this policy

This policy applies to all employees. It does not apply to casual workers, agency workers or contractors.

Aims of this policy

This policy aims to minimise the disruption caused by employee absence by setting clear guidelines on absence notification, by encouraging regular communication to assist employees to return to work as soon and as safely as possible, and by assisting managers to handle absences due to illness or injury in a fair, consistent and effective way.

The examples in this template policy are generic, but you can amend the content to suit your needs. Please be practical though, and include the underlined paragraphs as they are essential to ensure your compliance.

Time off for medical and dental appointments

Wherever possible, and in order to minimise disruption, employees are asked to make medical and dental appointments either outside of normal working hours, or at the beginning or end of the working day. However, we do realise that this may not always be possible, particularly with hospital appointments.

Employees who need to take time off to attend a medical or dental appointment should notify their manager, giving as much notice as possible. Such time off will paid but we do request that the time is made up.

Employees who have an appointment, which is not at the end of the working day, will normally be expected to return to work following the appointment

Absence notification

An employee who is unable to attend work for any reason should contact his/her manager as soon as possible but in any event no later than one hour after his/her normal start time on the first day of absence.

In order to minimise disruption it is important that we receive as much notice of absence as practically possible. An employee should always endeavour to notify us personally. However in the event that the employee has an illness or situation that absolutely prevents them contacting us personally they should ensure that a relative, neighbour or friend contacts us on his/her behalf. In addition, the reason for the absence and an indication of its likely duration should be provided. The reason for the absence will be kept confidential if this is requested.

See below regarding sickness whilst absent from work on authorised holiday, or just prior to taking authorised holiday. Absent employees are then responsible to keep their manager informed of their situation on a regular basis. They should remain in contact with us, and if away from home at any time during their absence, should provide us with full contact details. We may contact them during a period of absence and, in addition, may visit them at home to discuss their health and progress towards returning to work.

An employee who is absent through sickness or injury for more than one week must obtain a Statement of Fitness for Work from a doctor and forward it to their manager. The name of the doctor, the surgery and its contact information should be clearly stated. If a period of medically certified absence is extended by a further Statement, your manager must be informed on the same day and advised of the extension of the absence.

If a Statement of Fitness for Work indicates that the employee is unable to undertake the full duties of his/her normal job, but may be able to do some work, we will discuss this with him/her and consider any recommendations or suggestions made by the GP which may facilitate an earlier return to work.

On return to work after absence, all employees are required to complete a self-certification of absence/return to work form covering the complete period of absence, irrespective of whether a Statement of Fitness for Work was submitted. Your manager will discuss the details with you and will counter-sign the form (provided the information provided is satisfactory) indicating whether or not payment is to be made for the period of absence. This form will then be retained on the employee's personnel file, and payroll notified of any payment implications.

Sick pay will not normally be paid for any absences that are due to reasons other than the employee's own illness/injury.

Whilst absent from work due to illness or injury, employees must not take on any other work, either paid or unpaid, without our consent, irrespective of whether sick pay is still being paid. Employees remain bound by all of the terms and conditions of their contracts of employment. If therapeutic work is recommended, we should be informed and we will take any appropriate steps to provide this ourselves, if practicable.

Failure to comply with the above procedures could affect any entitlement to sick pay and, in some instances, could warrant disciplinary action.

Sick pay and benefits

Contractual sick pay will normally be paid for absences owing to illness or accident, up to a maximum period as outlined in the employee's contract of employment and will include any Statutory Sick Pay (SSP) payable for that period. The maximum period of entitlement (which may be made up of one or more periods of absence) will be calculated on a rolling 12-month basis. The entitlement to sick pay will be calculated as at the first date of absence in the current absence period, deducting any sick pay paid in the twelve month period prior to that date.

For clarification, once the total maximum entitlement has been exhausted, it will not be recalculated during the current absence, irrespective of its duration or irrespective of any increased length of service.

Employees who exhaust their entitlement to contractual sick pay may still be entitled to receive SSP (see below). Sick pay for part-time employees will be on a pro-rata basis to the full-time normal working week.

Payment of contractual sick pay depends on us being satisfied that the sick pay system is not being abused. Failure to report the reason for absence or to maintain regular contact could result in non-payment, as could repeated instances of short-term absence (where there appears to be no underlying medical reason for these), or failure to attend an occupational health appointment if this is requested.

Contractual sick pay will not normally be paid during any notice period (irrespective of whether the notice is given by the employee or by us), nor during any absence due to sickness during the course of disciplinary proceedings or during investigations into alleged breaches of our rules, procedures or contractual obligations.

The entitlement to sick pay may also be affected if notification of absence is later than the end of the first qualifying day of absence.

In the event of the self-certification of absence form not being countersigned by your manager, the absence will be treated as unauthorised and payment of contractual sick pay will be withheld.

An employee who feels that his/her payment has been unfairly withheld should use our grievance procedure.

Any benefits under the contract of employment will normally continue to be provided during any period of absence lasting less than 13 weeks. After this time we reserve the right to ask for the return of any company equipment or company vehicle which we may need in the employee's absence.

Statutory leave will continue to accrue during periods of long-term sick, contractual leave in excess of this will cease to accrue after 13 weeks' absence and will only start to accrue again on return to work.

Statutory Sick Pay (SSP)

Employees are entitled to SSP provided they meet the detailed requirements of the scheme. They cannot get SSP if they are not sick for four or more days in a row as this does not form a period of incapacity for work' (PIW). The following categories of employee are excluded from receiving SSP, if:

- *their average weekly earnings are less than the lower earnings limit for National Insurance contributions*

- *they have already had 28 weeks' worth of SSP from us and this new spell of sickness links to the last one*

- *they were not entitled to SSP the last time he/she was sick, for any reason, and this spell of sickness links to that one*

- *they started or returned to work after getting Employment and Support Allowance (ESA) from the JobCentre Plus and are a 'benefit recipient' who is sick within the first 104 weeks of starting, or returning to, work for us*

- *they had a series of linked PIWs lasting more than three years*

- *they have not done any work for us under their contract of employment*

- *they are away sick during a stoppage of work due to a trade dispute which started before the first day of sickness, unless they have not taken part in the trade dispute and have no direct interest in it*

- *they are pregnant and the absence is either wholly or partly because of the pregnancy, and it occurs during the qualifying period for Statutory Maternity Pay (SMP) which commences with:*

  - *the beginning of the week they are first entitled to SMP or the fourth week before their expected week of confinement; or*

  - *the beginning of the week they are first entitled to Maternity Allowance (MA) from the Department for Work and Pensions (DWP); or*

  - *the beginning of the fourth week before their expected week of confinement if they cannot get SMP or MA*

  - *they are outside the EU and we are not liable to pay employer's Class 1 NICs, even if their earnings are high enough*

  - *they are in legal custody.*

Qualifying days for SSP

Unless otherwise specified in the employee's statement of terms and conditions or contract of employment, the days on which he/she would normally have worked had he/she not fallen sick will be identified as his/her qualifying days for SSP.

Waiting days

Employees are eligible for SSP on the fourth qualifying day in a 'period of incapacity for work' (PIW). The first three qualifying days are known as 'waiting days', and there is no entitlement to SSP for these days.

Linked periods of absence

Two or more continuous spells of sickness both lasting at least four days, which are separated by 56 calendar days or less, are linked together and counted as one. This means that an employee who has already had three waiting days in a period of incapacity, and then has a second linked spell within 56 days, will be paid SSP from the first qualifying day in the second spell.

Duration of payment

Provided the eligibility criteria are met, SSP is payable for up to 28 weeks of sickness absence in either:

- *one period of incapacity for work, or*

- *any number of periods linked by 56 calendar days (8 weeks) or less. These cannot extend for more than three years*

Amount of SSP

The government fixes the rate of SSP, which is normally reviewed annually. To be entitled to SSP the employee must earn at least the equivalent of Class One National Insurance Lower Earnings limit. SSP is subject to Income Tax and National Insurance deductions. The amount of SSP will be shown on the employee's payslip

Return to work after absence

It is important to explain to your employee the procedure to follow on their return to work. This will provide managers with a process to follow, and ensure all staff are treated consistently and fairly.

It is our policy that all employees are seen on their return to work, informally, by their manager as soon as possible. The reasons for the absence will be discussed in appropriate detail depending on the nature and frequency of the absence(s).

The employee will also be briefed on any developments in his/her area of work which occurred during the absence. The manager will discuss the workload and how best to minimise any disruption that may have been caused by the absence. He or she will also need to know whether the employee is fully fit to return or should refrain from any tasks for health reasons.

An employee who, for whatever reason, finds it difficult to discuss the reasons for absence with his/her manager, or who prefers to speak to a manager of the same sex, should ask for this and we will make every effort to comply.

If a phased return to work has been agreed, payment will depend on the circumstances and the duration of the part-time working arrangement. If contractual sick pay is exhausted, the employee will normally be paid for any hours worked at his/her normal basic hourly rate during a phased return (subject to earning at least the rate of SSP where there is an entitlement to this). If contractual sick pay is not exhausted, this will continue to be paid and the shortfall between worked hours and normal working hours will be deducted from the sick pay entitlement. If the employee is being paid SSP only, this will be the minimum rate of pay whilst on a phased return to work programme, unless SSP is exhausted, in which case payment will only be made for the actual hours worked.

An employee who wishes to continue with the reduced or revised hours indefinitely should ask his/her manager to consider a permanent change to the contract of employment and we will discuss the implications of this with him/her

If a phased return to work has been agreed, payment will depend on the circumstances and the duration of the part-time working arrangement. If contractual sick pay is exhausted, the employee will normally be paid for any hours worked at his/her normal basic hourly rate during a phased return (subject to earning at least the rate of SSP where there is an entitlement to this). If contractual sick pay is not exhausted, this will continue to be paid and the shortfall between worked hours and normal working hours will be deducted from the sick pay entitlement. _If the employee is being paid SSP only, this will be the minimum rate of pay whilst on a phased return to work programme, unless SSP is exhausted, in which case payment will only be made for the actual hours worked._

An employee who wishes to continue with the reduced or revised hours indefinitely should ask his/her manager to consider a permanent change to the contract of employment and we will discuss the implications of this with him/her.

Medical reports

It is important that you follow this process correctly if you are including it in your policy.

We reserve the right, at any time during employment, to require an employee to attend an independent medical examination, or to ask permission to contact his/her doctor or consultant for a report.

Prior written consent will be requested before we approach any doctor or consultant who is treating the employee, and full details will be provided of the employee's rights and obligations under the Access to Medical Reports Act.

We would normally request such a report in the following circumstances: where an employee complains of an ongoing health problem which is affecting his/her ability to do his/her job; where an employee claims that any aspect of his/her job is creating a health problem; where the absence gives us cause for concern; where an employee has been absent for some time and there is doubt about when he/she may be able to return to work.

We may also request a medical report if we are considering dismissal for either a long-term health problem or unsatisfactory attendance made up of repeated short absences. In addition, if an employee has any health problem that could be considered a disability we would wish to seek a report in order to obtain guidance on what, if any, reasonable adjustments should be made to enable the employee to perform his/her duties satisfactorily.

Employees are required to co-operate with our procedures, including providing medical advice and ensuring we are kept informed of any developments in their treatment or condition.

In addition to the above, we have contracted external occupational health advisors whom we may ask to advise us generally, and also to assist with the rehabilitation of those returning after lengthy absences or following serious illness or injury.

Our standard employment contracts contain a clause requiring that employees co-operate with us by attending any occupational health assessments organised for them. Failure or *refusal to do so would be a breach of contract and could also lead to any contractual sick pay being withdrawn.*

Excessive absenteeism

The wording of this section is crucial to protect the company from abuse of the system.

Employees who have a number of short absences that together comprise an unacceptable overall level of absence will be seen by their manager to discuss the frequency and reasons for these absences. This will be done in accordance with our disciplinary procedure, on grounds of unsatisfactory attendance, and will apply irrespective of whether the absences are believed to be genuine or not. The manager will explain what we consider to be an "acceptable" level of attendance. What is "acceptable" may be different depending on the nature of the work, the ability of the department to provide cover, the employee's length of service, previous absence history, the reasons given for the absences and the treatment of other employees in similar situations. If, despite warnings, attendance remains unsatisfactory, this may result in dismissal. Prior to dismissal, the employee will be invited to attend a formal meeting to discuss his/her attendance. He/she may be accompanied at this meeting by a colleague or a trade union representative. The reasons for the absence, and the individual's overall level of attendance, will be fully discussed. If a decision is taken to dismiss, this will be confirmed in writing, together with details of any right of appeal and our appeals procedure.

Long-term sickness

You need to give this section careful consideration, and only include clauses that you know you can, and will, deliver. Let's say, for example, you state that you will send all employees who are on long term sick leave for more than four weeks to see an independent GP. But then the situation arises and you decide against it because it is too expensive. This will not only give the message that the policies are not being followed, but also leave them open to abuse in the future, making it difficult for you to follow in future cases, as this will be perceived as being inconsistent and/or unfair.

We will normally make arrangements to see employees who are absent from work for a period in excess of 6 weeks. This may be either at work or at their home, to update ourselves on their progress and to ask for permission to obtain a doctor's or consultant's report. Employees may refuse their permission, but it should be emphasised that the request is made to help us manage the situation and it will usually be to their advantage to enable us to get further information about their likely date of return to work, whether any medical restrictions should be placed on their activities, and whether they have any condition which would be classed as a disability.

We will aim to inform an employee who is about to exhaust his/her entitlement to either SSP or company sick pay of this.

Employees may, if they choose, request to take some annual leave during periods of sickness absence, or prior to returning to work. Employees who are unable to take at least their statutory holiday entitlement during our holiday year (including any bank/public holidays taken as paid leave) may carry the shortfall forward into the next holiday year, provided that they have adhered to our sickness reporting procedure and have provided required documentation where applicable. Statutory leave will continue to accrue during periods of long-term sick, contractual leave in excess of this will cease to accrue after 13 weeks' absence and will only start to accrue again on return to work.

If the absence continues at a level that we deem unacceptable, or if it becomes evident that there is little likelihood of a return to work, we will reassess the situation and may take a decision to dismiss on grounds of ill-health.

If dismissal is being considered, we will write to the employee, giving advance notice of a formal meeting to discuss the situation. The employee may, if he/she wishes, be accompanied at this meeting by a colleague or a trade union representative.

Before reaching a decision, we will take into account the nature of the illness, any advice we have received from a doctor, consultant or occupational health professional as to likely return to work and future capabilities, length of service, previous absence history and performance. If the absence is due to a reason related to a disability, we will also wish to explore any ways of accommodating this.

If a decision is taken to dismiss, this will be confirmed in writing, together with the details of any right of appeal and our appeals procedure.

Health concerns and contact with infectious and contagious diseases

An employee who suspects that he/she may be suffering from, or who is diagnosed as suffering from, any condition which may affect his/her ability to do his/her job is required to notify their manager in order that we may take all reasonable steps to ensure his/her well-being at work.

Any employee who has been in contact with an infectious or contagious disease (including diphtheria, typhoid, paratyphoid, polio or tuberculosis), should report the fact immediately to their manager and then obtain advice as to whether it is necessary to remain away from work. Such absence will be treated as paid sick leave.

An employee who has been in contact with measles, mumps, whooping cough, German measles (rubella) or chicken pox need not normally remain away from work

Accidents whilst at work

> **This paragraph is worded to comply with this document only. Please note that you should have a full explanation regarding how to manage accidents at work in your Health and Safety Policy. On its own, this paragraph will not be enough.**

The details of any absence that is related in any way to an accident at work should be recorded in our accident book, which is situated in the main office, and you should also notify your manager.

Sickness whilst on holiday

> **This is often a highly contentious point for employees and managers alike. Having clear guidelines will avoid tension should it arise. However, it is important to ensure all your managers are following the policy, as nothing upsets staff more than inconsistency.**

An employee who falls sick either prior to commencing planned holiday absence, or during a period of paid holiday, <u>and would otherwise be unable to take at least his/her statutory holiday entitlement under the Working Time Regulations in this holiday year (including any bank/public holidays taken as paid holiday), may request that the period of illness during the authorised holiday is converted to sick leave and the holiday taken at a later date.</u>

In this case, the employee is required to phone his/her manager on each day of the illness to confirm that he/she is ill and, if entitled to contractual sick pay during this period, provide a medical certificate covering the total period of the absence." Note that self-certification may suffice for SSP but is not regarded as sufficient for the payment of contractual sick pay whilst absent on pre-authorised holiday.

An employee who falls sick on a working day directly before or after a bank or public holiday, or directly following absence for authorised holiday, will be required to produce a medical certificate in order to qualify for contractual sick pay

Emergency time off for dependants

There is specific legislation covering time off to care for dependants, and it is wise not to visit this in this policy unless you are absolutely sure of the wording. The paragraph below is intended to provide guidance on differentiating between employee sickness, and leave to look after sick dependants.

This absence policy and payment schemes relate to absence due to the employee's own illness or injury, not that of other members of their family or dependants. Reasonable time off will be authorised to deal with the urgent unforeseen needs of a dependant, but this will normally be unpaid

Elective surgery

With the increase in cosmetic surgery, and non-essential medical procedures, it is important to provide guidance to staff on your company position. This will avoid confusion. Be careful if using the phrase *manager's discretion* as this can often provide inconsistency and may lead to conflict. I have put in a discretionary clause, but have carefully worded it to ensure that no unilateral decision is made, and that it doesn't include certain types of procedure.

For the purposes of this policy, elective surgery is surgery that is not considered to be medically necessary or surgery for non-medical reasons. Examples might include vasectomies, the removal of bunions and the removal of warts. This provision is not intended to cover surgical or non-surgical procedures that are concerned solely with the enhancement of physical appearance (e.g. face lifts, breast enlargements, facial peels, teeth whitening, dental veneers etc) for which time away from work should be taken from holiday entitlement or as time off in lieu.

We accept that there may be circumstances where a manager wishes to exercise his/her discretion to allow time off for elective surgery depending on the individual circumstances. The employee making the request should discuss the reason for the time off and the underlying circumstances with his/her manager who may after discussion with a senior member of staff authorise up to five day's paid leave in any one year for an employee to undergo elective surgery.

Time off in excess of this should be taken as either annual leave, time off in lieu (TOIL) or unpaid leave.

An employee who wishes to take time off for elective surgery is required to:

- *inform his/her manager as soon as the plans have been confirmed*

- *provide a statement from a qualified medical practitioner that elective surgery has been approved and giving the likely duration of recovery*

- *where possible, arrange for the elective surgery at a time that will cause the minimum amount of inconvenience to the company.*

- *provide as much notice as possible of the day on which the surgery will take place.*

Any information provided to your manager will be maintained in strict confidence. The reason for the employee's absence will be disclosed only on a "need-to-know" basis and in consultation with the employee.

Where the outcome of the surgery is unexpected and the employee suffers an injury or illness, our standard sick pay provisions will apply, following receipt of the relevant sickness certificate.

Fertility treatment

There isn't any legislation that says you have to allow time off for fertility treatment, should you decide to do so you must ensure you abide by your Equal Opportunities Policy.

We will grant up to five days paid leave in any one year (pro rata for part-time employees) for an employee to undergo fertility treatment. The policy applies equally to an employee whose partner is undergoing fertility treatment.

Any time off in excess of this should be taken as annual leave or, alternatively, unpaid leave may be authorised or a form of temporary flexible working may be approved, subject to the needs of the company.

Any employee who may need time off work for fertility treatment should inform his/her manager as soon as the plans have been confirmed; provide a statement from a qualified medical practitioner that fertility treatment has been recommended and approved; and, if requested, produce an appointment card for each occasion on which time off is required. Where possible, appointments should be made for times that will cause the minimum disruption to the working day, and we do ask that the employee provides as much notice as possible of the days and times on which time off is required.

Any information provided will be maintained in strict confidence.

Absence records and monitoring

The following paragraph is essential, and much of it is a legal requirement.

Details of an employee's health, either physical or mental, are categorised as "sensitive personal data" under the Data Protection Act. Health records are therefore kept in a secure filing cabinet in the (state where kept) office.

A record for each employee is kept, detailing the number of days absent, dates and reasons given.

These records are kept by the (state who is responsible for keeping these files). The employee and his/her manager may request to see the individual details at any time by following the correct procedure.

Our overall absence figures and the reasons for these will be reviewed and analysed by the senior management team on a regular basis to identify any trends or any areas of concern. Where areas of concern are highlighted, action will be taken to try to identify the causes and take appropriate action.

Related policies

We also have the following related policies:

- *Maternity, Paternity and Adoption*
- *Annual Leave Policy*
- *Equal Opportunities Policy*

Implementation, monitoring and review of this policy

Finish off with the date the policy comes into effect, and who has overall responsibility for the implementation and monitoring of the policy. In most companies this is a Director or Operations Manager. Also, you might include the date the policy will be reviewed. This is a standard paragraph which you'll need in other policies too.

This policy will take effect from (date). The (named person) has overall responsibility for implementing and monitoring this policy, which will be reviewed on a regular basis following its implementation and may be changed from time to time.

Any queries or comments about this policy should be addressed to the (named person).

3: Annual Leave Policy

You need to be specific when it comes to annual leave. Your Annual Leave Policy should cover the finer details of what is expected of staff, and give guidance on how, and when, they must book their leave. See *Do it Yourself HR Basics for Small Business* for templates of a booking leave form.

Your Company Name:

Referred to in this policy as "The Company"

Introduction

It is the policy of The Company to ensure that all staff receive an extended period of leisure time. However; to ensure the smooth running of the business, and to avoid unnecessary disruption caused by employee absence, this policy outlines the process to follow so we can ensure minimum staffing levels at all times.

Scope of this policy

This policy applies to all staff employed directly by The Company. It does not apply to casual workers, agency workers or contractors.

Aims of this policy

The aim of this policy is to set out the rules relating to annual leave, including the way in which leave is calculated, carrying over of leave, the affect of sickness on annual leave and enforced shut down periods.

Annual leave entitlement

Always cross-reference the policy with the employee's contract of employment. Make the entitlement clear, and put in a sentence about what happens if a new employee starts or leaves part way through the year.

Your basic annual leave entitlement can be found in your Contract of Employment.

Entitlement to paid holiday accrues throughout the year. If you join or leave our employment during the holiday year, your holiday entitlement for that year will be calculated on a pro-rata basis, rounded up to the nearest half-day.

Part time workers

Explain how you intend to calculate holidays for part time workers, and keep it as simple as possible.

If you work part-time, your holiday entitlement will be calculated on a pro-rata basis, based on your contractual hours. The calculation will include any allowance for bank holidays.

The annual leave year

Explain when the annual leave year starts, and take this opportunity to be more explicit about how the year is divided for starters and leavers.

The annual leave year runs from January 1st to December 31st each year. Employees starting part way through the year will have their annual leave calculated on a pro rata basis from the date they started until the end of the leave year. For the purpose of calculation anyone starting before the 15th of the month will receive full allowance for that month. If you started after the 15th of the month you will only receive half the allowance.

Annual leave during probationary period

All employees are entitled to annual leave, but the allowance during probation can be capped in line with statutory minimum requirements. You may also add a clause to say that annual leave is not normally permitted during the probationary or induction period.

An employee on probation will accrue annual leave as set out in the Contract of Employment. However, unless agreed prior to starting employment annual leave will not normally be allowed during the first month of employment. This is to ensure the employee has a full induction into their role and a smooth handover (if relevant).

Enforced annual leave

If your company shuts down during Christmas, for example, or during other holiday periods, you can include a clause advising staff that they must keep enough leave for this shutdown period. At this point take the opportunity to explain the company's view on taking leave the day prior to a shutdown. This avoids fall-out caused by staff complaining if the company decides to close early and they had booked a full day's leave.

You must ensure that you keep sufficient leave to cover local bank holidays, summer and Christmas shut down periods. Please note that if staff book annual leave on the day prior to a shut down period and the company decide to close down half way through the day, the company will not reimburse staff for that half day. Staff will be notified of shut down periods at the beginning of the holiday year.

Unused annual leave

Another important area to get right is being consistent with unused leave. It is the **employer's** responsibility to ensure that staff take their minimum statutory entitlement. However, if the company provides holiday leave in excess of the minimum requirement it should be clear whether these days have to be used. If they are not used, can they be carried over, paid in cash, or are they lost? Your decision.

Except for exceptional circumstances annual leave cannot be carried over from one year to another, with the exception of <u>staff on long term sickness who have not had the opportunity to use up all their leave entitlement</u>. Payment in lieu of leave not taken will not be granted. Any leave not taken will be forfeited.

Sickness prior, during or following annual leave

As per your Absence and Sickness Policy, you should enter a paragraph stating what happens in the event of sickness prior to, during, or immediately after, annual leave.

An employee who falls sick either prior to commencing planned holiday absence, or during a period of paid holiday, and would otherwise be unable to take at least his/her statutory holiday entitlement under the Working Time Regulations in this holiday year (including any bank/public holidays taken as paid holiday), may request that the period of illness during the authorised holiday is converted to sick leave and the holiday taken at a later date. Note that self-certification may suffice for SSP but is not regarded as sufficient for the payment of contractual sick pay whilst absent on pre-authorised holiday. Therefore a medical certificate covering the total period of absence will be required.

An employee who falls sick on a working day directly before or after a bank or public holiday, or directly following absence for authorised holiday, will be required to produce a medical certificate in order to qualify for contractual sick pay

Please see the Absence & Sickness Policy for further information.

Religious holidays

Whether or not you have a culturally diverse workforce you should still include a paragraph stating what the company recognises as religious holidays. This may avoid claims of discrimination in the future.

Employees who wish to observe religious holidays that do not coincide with the recognised public holidays in England and Wales are required to use their annual leave or take unpaid leave. Every effort will be made to accommodate such requests, which will be refused only in exceptional circumstances.

Varying hours of work

Life changes mean that employees may, from time to time, need to vary their hours of work. Even if you only have full time staff working for you at present, you should still include a paragraph on how the company will allocate leave should a variation of hours occur.

If an employee changes from full time to part-time working, or vice-versa, part way through a leave year the leave allowance for that year will be adjusted on a pro rated basis in accordance with the contracted hours.

Requesting annual leave

There are certain times of the year when the majority of people will probably want to be home from work, e.g. Christmas, or school holidays. This can be a problem, particularly if you are a small employer, or run a seasonal business which requires staffing at these times. Make it clear how you will prioritise requests for annual leave. It could be on a rota basis or a first-come basis. Below is an example of how you can cover this issue.

A request for annual leave will only be considered on submission of an annual leave request form. The form must be completed and handed to your manager. Your manager will consider requests for annual leave on a first come, first served basis. Please do not book annual leave prior to arranging it with your manager, as the company cannot be responsible for holidays booked without the necessary permission. Managers are responsible for ensuring that all leave is recorded and entered on the annual leave calendar.

If you leave us

Make it clear how you calculate leave in the event of an employee resigning or being dismissed. Ensure your policy complies with legislation. Below is an example of how you should calculate leave under these circumstances.

Should you leave our employment any leave outstanding will be calculated on a pro rated basis up to your last day of employment. We reserve the right to refuse annual leave during your notice period. If you have exceeded your leave entitlement any overpayment will be deducted from your final salary.

If your employment is terminated due to gross misconduct, or you fail to serve your statutory notice, annual leave will only be calculated up to and including your last day of work.

Related policies

We also have the following related policies:

- *Maternity, Paternity and Adoption Policy*
- *Absence & Sickness Policy*
- *Equal Opportunities Policy*

Implementation, monitoring and review of this policy

This policy will take effect from (date). (Named person) has overall responsibility for implementing and monitoring this policy, which will be reviewed on a regular basis following its implementation and may be changed from time to time.

Any queries or comments about this policy should be addressed to (named person).

4: Grievance Policy

Some companies have a combined Disciplinary and Grievance Policy. This is acceptable, but personally I believe they should be kept separate. A grievance procedure provides individuals with a course of action if they have a complaint (which they are unable to resolve through regular communication with their line manager). Whereas a disciplinary procedure is often seen as a guide to let employees know what is expected of them in terms of standards of performance or conduct (and the likely consequences of continued failure to meet these standards).

Your Company Name:

Referred to in this policy as "The Company"

Introduction

Our grievance procedure is designed to ensure that any questions and problems at work are quickly aired and resolved fairly and consistently, and we therefore encourage its use.

This procedure is non-contractual but is designed to indicate how such matters should be dealt with within The Company although we reserve the right at our discretion to vary, replace or terminate the procedure at any stage.

All managers are reminded of the requirement to comply with the ACAS Code of Practice on Disciplinary and Grievance Procedures and to take all steps to ensure that any grievance is handled both fairly and reasonably.

Scope of this procedure

This procedure covers all employees and workers, including those on casual contracts. It does not apply to agency workers or self-employed contractors

Aims of this procedure

This procedure aims to encourage the early resolution of any work-related issues, and to ensure that these are resolved fairly and consistently. Grievances may relate to action which has already been taken or which is contemplated in relation to an employee or worker, or may include the actions of third parties such as colleagues. They may relate to a wide range of issues including terms and conditions of employment, health and safety, work relations, new working practices, working environment, organisational change or equal opportunities issues.

The focus of the grievance procedure is to achieve resolution, not to apportion blame.

Stages of the procedure

Once you are clear about the aims of the procedure it is essential to provide clearly defined stages that the grievance process will follow. It is essential that the employee understands the seriousness of following this action, and what will be involved once the process is initiated. It is always better to try and resolve an issue informally if at all possible.

Our grievance procedure enables any grievances to be raised and settled as quickly and as near to the point of origin as possible. Clearly many issues will, and indeed should, be resolved informally without the need for the formal procedure. However should an informal approach not result in the required resolution, the procedure set out below should be used

Stage one

If you have a grievance relating to your employment, and you have not been able to resolve this informally, please set out in writing the details of your grievance, giving the full grounds for your complaint and details of the resolution being sought, and send this to your manager (unless you are a senior manager or director, in which case the Managing Director).

Your letter should be dated and should state that you are raising a formal grievance under our grievance procedure. <u>We will respond to you and will meet with you to hear your grievance.</u> <u>At this meeting you will be given full opportunity to state your case.</u> After giving full consideration to the points you have raised, and having undertaken any further investigation we consider to be appropriate, we will then confirm the outcome in writing to you, confirming any action we intend to take to resolve the grievance, together with your right to appeal against this outcome.

Your appeal should be received by the nominated person within seven calendar days of receipt of our letter

Stage two

Failing a satisfactory solution at stage one, you may appeal to the manager directly senior to your manager (unless you are a senior manager or director, in which case the Board of Directors). Again you should do this in writing if possible.

The person hearing your appeal will arrange to meet with you as soon as is reasonably practicable to discuss your grievance and again you will be given full opportunity to state your case. He or she will attempt to resolve the matter to the satisfaction of both parties. Whatever decision is taken by him or her will be final and will be confirmed to you in writing.

Should your grievance relate to the behaviour or decisions made by your manager him/herself, then please raise the matter, as soon as possible, at stage two. In this case if the person hearing your grievance is unable to resolve it to your satisfaction, you will have the right of appeal, which will be to a further senior manager if practicable.

Once a decision has been made to file a grievance it is essential your guidelines are followed. Below are examples that will help your process go as smoothly as possible. When writing your guidelines ensure they are relevant to your company, as generic clauses will confuse the issue if they are irrelevant.

Guidelines

Grievances should be raised and the above procedure followed without unreasonable delay at any stage.

At all formal stages of this procedure, the person hearing a grievance is advised to be accompanied by a suitable employee of The Company who will act as a witness and take full notes of everything that is said. Where no internal person of sufficient seniority or confidential status is available, or where preferred, an external party may be invited to attend in this capacity.

At all stages of this procedure the individual raising the grievance may choose to be accompanied by either a fellow worker, a trade union representative (who must be certified in writing by the union as having experience of, or having received training in, acting as a worker's companion at disciplinary or grievance hearings) or an official employed by a trade union.

The employee or worker raising the grievance should tell the person conducting the hearing in advance whom he/she has chosen as a companion. It would not normally be reasonable to insist on being accompanied by someone whose presence would prejudice the hearing nor would it be reasonable to ask to be accompanied by someone from a remote geographical site if someone suitable and willing is available on site.

The companion is there to act as a witness to what was said, to provide moral support and to assist and advise the person in presenting his/her case. He or she may address the meeting (provided the person wishes this), ask questions on his/her behalf and confer with the individual raising the grievance but not answer questions on his/her behalf. The companion is also not permitted to prevent us from explaining our case.

Fellow workers may not be compelled to attend as a companion.

The individual raising the grievance should make every effort to attend the meeting. If however he/she or his/her chosen companion is unable to attend any meeting under this procedure for a reason which was not foreseeable at the time the meeting was arranged, we will attempt to rearrange the meeting for a date within five days of the original scheduled date.

The timing and location of meetings will be reasonable and we will aim to ensure that the procedure is followed without unreasonable delay. Meetings will be confidential, and wherever possible will be held in a private location and without interruptions.

At the grievance meeting, the individual raising the grievance will be invited to re-state the grievance and explain how he/she would like it to be resolved. Full opportunity will be provided to present any information and answer questions before any decision is made. The manager conducting the meeting may adjourn the meeting at any stage in order to calm a tense situation, to check out facts or take advice.

Reasonable adjustments will be made to ensure that any disabled individual is not disadvantaged in any way at the meeting. He/she should inform us of any particular requirements (eg for a signer or other support) where necessary. Arrangements may also be made to assist any person who does not have English as his or her first language and who may need an interpreter.

To ensure that any issue raised is resolved effectively, all parties should adhere to the following guidelines:

- *make sure you are clear about the facts and ignore rumours or hearsay*

- limit the issue to those involved and show discretion at all times

- work only to resolve the issue and actively pursue a positive outcome

- be honest about your own role and involvement

- demonstrate understanding, empathy and flexibility to ensure that the other person's perspective is accommodated

- strengthen relationships once the outcome is known and positively apply any learning points for the future.

When considering a suitable resolution, the person hearing the grievance will consider whether similar grievances have been raised before, how they have been resolved and any follow-up action that was taken.

Notes will be made of all meetings held under the grievance procedure, with one copy being given to the person raising the grievance and one being kept on file. *Such documents will be regarded as confidential.*

In summary, any employee or worker who has an issue, however small, which he/she has been unable to resolve informally, should raise it as soon as possible, using the above procedure, in order that we may deal with it fairly and quickly.

An employee or worker who believes that he/she is subject to conduct or capability related disciplinary action which is unlawfully discriminatory, or who feels that the action is being taken for reasons other than conduct or capability, should use this grievance procedure rather than appealing within the disciplinary procedure. In such cases, the disciplinary process will normally be suspended whilst the grievance is investigated and resolved

Former employees

There may be occasions when a complaint is raised by an employee that has left your company. It is important to have a clause in your Grievance Procedure that states complaints relating to dismissals must be dealt with via the Disciplinary Procedure. Below is an example of the wording.

If the complaint relates to dissatisfaction with a dismissal decision, an appeal should be made against that decision in accordance with the appeal process set out in our disciplinary procedure, rather than invoking the grievance procedure.

Related policies

We also have the following related policies:

- Disciplinary Policy

- Equal Opportunities Policy

Implementation, monitoring and review of this procedure

This procedure will take effect from (date). (Named person) has overall responsibility for implementing and monitoring this procedure, which will be reviewed on a regular basis following its implementation and may be changed from time to time.

Any queries or comments about this procedure should be addressed to (Named person).

5: Maternity / Paternity / Adoption Policy

I was once told by a director of a small business that he didn't need this policy because he didn't intend employing anyone that could fall into the category. Apart from the obvious breach of equal opportunities, the majority of working people could be eligible under one of these categories. It is common for this policy to be most relevant to women under 45 who may start a family. However, the reality is that current legislation also affords considerable rights to working fathers and couples (mixed and single-sex), who are seeking to adopt.

Because this policy covers such a wide subject, it is simpler and clearer to break it down into three sections, although it is common practice for the first section to cover maternity. Ensure that you write this policy so it also covers the procedure as it can then be used by both managers and staff as an at a glance guide through the process.

Your Company Name:

Referred to in this policy as "The Company"

Introduction

All employees have the right not to suffer any detriment on the grounds of pregnancy, childbirth, or for taking maternity, adoption or paternity leave. This right applies in relation to both an act and a failure to act.

We comply with all statutory requirements and offer benefits which are in line with the statutory benefits scheme.

This policy is not contractual but sets out the way in which we plan to manage maternity, adoption and paternity leave.

Scope of this policy

This policy covers all employees, including those on fixed-term contracts, who meet the eligibility requirements for statutory leave and pay.

Aims of this policy

This policy aims to set out our procedures for taking family leave and to ensure that employees are aware of their entitlements. An employee who has any questions about this policy or about any other aspect of his/her statutory entitlements should contact their manager.

Maternity - time off for ante-natal care

There are quite specific rules to follow with regards to maternity, but before starting this section take time to think about your procedure. Ensure that any guidelines are in line with your other policies e.g. Sickness and Absence Policy. Start at the very beginning – from the time the employee advises that they are pregnant.

Pregnant employees are entitled to take time off during normal working hours to receive ante-natal care, although wherever possible appointments should be arranged at the start or end of the working day. Ante-natal care includes appointments with the GP, hospital clinics and relaxation classes.

Employees should advise their manager of any absence as far in advance of the appointment as possible, and, following the first appointment, may be asked to produce an appointment card.

There will be no deduction of pay for attending authorised ante-natal appointments. Employees receiving IVF treatment will be entitled to paid time off for ante-natal care only after the fertilised embryo has been implanted.

Maternity – leave

When it comes to maternity leave, avoid putting monetary figures in. If you do include any you will need to remember to change it every time the amounts change.

All employees are entitled to 52 weeks' statutory maternity leave, irrespective of their length of service or the number of hours worked each week. The first 26 weeks is known as "ordinary maternity leave" (OML); the second 26 weeks is known as "additional maternity leave" (AML). If an employee becomes pregnant again during maternity leave, she has the right to further ordinary and additional maternity leave.

If an employee loses her baby, but meets all other eligibility conditions, she can still take maternity leave if the baby is either stillborn after 24 weeks of pregnancy or born alive at any point of the pregnancy.

Maternity - commencing maternity leave

This is set in legislation, so take particular care not to change the wording of this section.

Maternity leave may begin at any time after the start of the 11th week before the week in which the child is due. The only exception to this is if the employee falls ill because of pregnancy at any time after the start of the fourth week before the child is due. In such circumstances, maternity leave will start on the first day of absence.

Maternity - notification requirements

The employee must notify us of her pregnancy, the expected date of her baby's birth, her intention to take maternity leave, and the date on which she intends this to start. This notification should be in writing and should be provided no later than the end of the 15th week before the expected week of childbirth. The employee should subsequently also provide a form MAT B1, signed by the doctor or midwife, confirming her pregnancy.

We will write to the employee to confirm receipt of her notification within 28 days of receiving this, and to confirm the date on which her maternity leave will end. This will normally be 52 weeks from the intended start date of her leave.

In exceptional circumstances notification can be given after the child is born but as a general rule failure to serve notice at the relevant time will mean the loss of the right to take maternity leave

Maternity - work and contact during the maternity leave period

The government has recently introduced Keeping in Touch days (KIT). This is to enable the employee to be kept aware of company news, issues and facts surrounding her workload. Again you should not amend the wording below.

A woman on maternity leave can work for a few days without losing her right to maternity leave or a week's statutory pay, via "keeping in touch" or KIT days. The number of days is limited to ten, irrespective of the length of maternity leave taken by the employee. KIT days may be taken at any time during the maternity leave period (excluding the first two compulsory maternity leave weeks), and may be taken singly or in blocks.

The employee and her manager should agree in advance what work will actually be done on KIT days. There is no obligation to work any KIT days and we are under no obligation to provide them. Payment will be agreed with the employee, noting that the minimum that must be paid for any week during the maternity pay period is the SMP rate to which the employee is entitled. Lower rate SMP may be offset against this.

Employees on maternity leave are encouraged to keep in touch with us and we will continue to make reasonable contact with them during their maternity leave

Maternity - returning from maternity leave

An employee now has far more choice on the amount of leave they take, and when they return. New legislation enables new mothers and fathers to transfer leave between themselves. This can prove complicated for small business owners in particular, and it is important that you follow the guidelines carefully to avoid complicating issues further.

The first two weeks after the birth must not be worked. This is referred to as 'compulsory maternity leave' and increases to four weeks for employees who work in a factory.

Employees who return to work at the end of their statutory maternity leave period do not need to notify us in advance of the date of return. However, we do request they keep in touch with us and notify us of any changes in their intentions as soon as possible.

If an employee wishes to return to work before the end of her statutory maternity leave period she must give us 56 days' (eight weeks) advance written notice specifying the date of return.

An employee who decides not to return to work at the end of her maternity leave is required to give full contractual notice.

Parents may choose to transfer the second six months of maternity leave to the father/partner, once the mother has returned to work. For further details, see below: 'Additional Statutory Paternity Leave'.

Please note that a mother who returns from maternity leave early, in order to enable her partner to take the remainder of the leave, must give her permission for us to release any information confirming her return to our employment and the period of her maternity leave and pay to her partner's employer, before we may do so. Such information will not be disclosed otherwise, which may result in delay in the partner receiving any remaining maternity pay or his/her ASPL being authorised by his/her employer.

Maternity – pay

Unless you intend to offer an advanced maternity package, keep the next section basic and following legislation guidelines. Don't be tempted to quote figures and ensure the information is accurate and current.

To qualify for Statutory Maternity Pay (SMP), employees must have at least 26 weeks' service extending into the 15th week before the week in which the baby is due (the 'qualifying week') and must have average earnings equal to, or greater than, the lower earnings limit for National Insurance contributions. SMP is payable whether or not the employee intends to return to work.

SMP is payable for a maximum of 39 weeks. Week one of the maternity pay period is the week after the employee leaves work or starts her maternity leave. To claim SMP the employee must give 28 days' written notice of when she wishes her SMP payments to commence.

The amount of SMP entitlement will vary depending upon earnings and the amount of maternity leave taken: the first six weeks are paid at 90% of average weekly earnings, followed by the lesser of either 90% of average earnings or the lower statutory weekly rate for up to 33 weeks. SMP is paid into the employee's bank account on the same date that pay would have been paid, and is subject to deductions for tax, National Insurance and pension contributions in the usual way.

Employees who do not qualify for SMP may be entitled to claim State Maternity Allowance.

Maternity - contractual benefits

With regards to company benefits, it is worth noting the benefits that need to be continued, and what benefits may change as a result. Below is a standard guide for you to follow.

Full holiday entitlement will continue to accrue throughout the period of maternity leave.

Other non-pay contractual benefits (such as a company vehicle, life or private health insurance, medical cover or childcare vouchers) will continue to be provided during the full period of maternity leave. The entire period of maternity leave will also be included when calculating the employee's length of service for the purposes of any contractual benefits.

Pension contributions will however be paid during the period of paid maternity leave only (up to 39 weeks), and will be based on the full pensionable pay the employee would receive if working.

An employee returning to work after ordinary maternity leave has the right to return to the same job.

The right to return following additional maternity leave is to the same job unless this is not reasonably practicable, but any alternative job must be both suitable and appropriate. The terms must be no less favourable than those which would have applied had the employee not been absent on maternity leave.

Maternity - risk assessments

Getting the next section right is essential for both the company and for the protection of the employee. You are obliged to provide suitable provisions for mothers should they decide to return to work whilst still breastfeeding their baby.

Immediately an employee notifies us of her pregnancy, a separate, individual risk assessment will be undertaken to ensure that all practicable measures are taken to prevent the risk of damage to the health or safety of the mother or her unborn child. Any employee who has concerns about her health and safety should raise these with her manager. In addition, we request that employees who return to work and who are breastfeeding notify us of this in order that suitable arrangements can be made to facilitate this.

Adoption - introduction

Adoption is now covered by legislation in much the same way as maternity.

One adoptive parent (of either sex) may be entitled to take up to 52 weeks' adoption leave. This is made up of 26 weeks' Ordinary Adoption Leave and 26 weeks' Additional Adoption Leave. Statutory Adoption Pay (SAP) is paid for up to 39 weeks, the remaining 13 weeks' (if taken) are unpaid. To qualify the employee must:

- *be the adopter of a child aged up to 18 years*

- *have at least 26 weeks' continuous employment extending into the 'matching week'. This is the week (beginning on a Sunday and ending on a Saturday) in which he/she is notified of having been matched with the child*

- *have notified the adoption agency that he/she agrees that the child should be placed with him/her, and on the date of placement.*

Only one person may take adoption leave in respect of a child at any time: where a couple is adopting a child jointly, one may take adoption leave and the other may take statutory paternity and/or additional statutory paternity leave (see below).

Adoption leave may begin on the actual date on which the child is placed with the employee, or it may start on a pre-determined date which falls within the period from 14 days before the child is placed until the expected date of the placement. If an employee is adopting a child from abroad, the leave may start on either the date the child enters the UK or a pre-determined date no later than 28 days after the date the child enters the UK. *Adoption leave can start on any day of the week.*

Adoption - notification requirements

The employee must give us notice of his/her intention to take statutory adoption leave, specifying the date of placement and the date on which he/she wishes to commence his/her leave. For the adoption of a child based in the UK, this must be given within seven days of the date on which he/she is notified of having been matched with the child. Documentary evidence which shows the name and address of the adoption agency, the name and date of birth of the child, date of notification of matching and the expected date of placement are also requested.

We will write to confirm our receipt of this notification within 28 days of receiving it, and confirming the date on which the statutory adoption leave will end. (This will normally be 52 weeks from the intended start date.)

The employee may vary the start date of the leave at a later date by giving us at least 28 days' notice.

Employees who are adopting a child from overseas should give written notice in three stages as follows:

1. Where the employee has 26 weeks' qualifying service, he/she should inform us within 28 days of receiving official notification of the date on which he/she received official notification of the placement and the date the child is expected to enter the UK. If the employee has less than 26 weeks' qualifying service, the notice should be given within 28 days of completing 26 weeks' service.

2. In all cases, the employee must give 28 days' notice of the actual date he/she wants the adoption leave to start. (For adoptions from abroad, this cannot be before the child enters the UK.) This date can be changed by giving at least 28 days' notice (or as soon as is reasonably practicable). We will write to confirm receipt of this notification within 28 days of receiving it.

3. The employee must tell us the date the child entered the UK within 28 days of the entry.

Adoption - length of adoption leave

Statutory adoption leave lasts for up to 52 weeks.

Adoption - contractual benefits

Full holiday entitlement will continue to accrue throughout the period of adoption leave.

Other non-pay contractual benefits (such as a company vehicle, life or private health insurance, medical cover or childcare vouchers) will continue to be provided during the full period of adoption leave. The entire period of adoption leave will also be included when calculating the employee's length of service for the purposes of any contractual benefits.

Pension contributions will however be paid during the period of paid adoption leave only (up to 39 weeks), and will be based on the full pensionable pay the employee would receive if working.

An employee returning to work after ordinary adoption leave has the right to return to the same job. The right to return following additional adoption leave is to the same job unless this is not reasonably practicable, but any alternative job must be both suitable and *appropriate. The terms must be no less favourable than those which would have applied had the employee not been absent on adoption leave.*

Adoption - work and contact during the adoption leave period

Those on adoption leave are able to work for a few days without losing their right to adoption leave or a week's statutory pay, via "keeping in touch" or KIT days. See maternity section above.

Adoption – pay

Statutory Adoption Pay is paid at the lesser of either 90% of normal weekly earnings or the fixed weekly rate during the first 39 weeks' of adoption leave. The remaining 13 weeks are unpaid

Adoption - notification of return

If the employee intends to return to work at the end of the ordinary or additional adoption leave, he/she need do nothing further. If however, the employee wishes to return to work earlier than this, at least 56 days' (eight weeks) notice of the date of intended return must be given. If the employee fails to give the minimum 56 days' notice we may postpone his/her return until 56 days' notice has been given.

Any employee who wishes to change his/her working pattern or hours on return from adoption leave must apply to do so following the statutory procedure for requesting flexible working arrangements.

Parents who adopt a child may transfer up to six months of adoption leave to the father/partner, once the primary adopter has returned to work. For further details, see below: 'Additional Statutory Paternity Leave'.

Please note that an employee who returns from adoption leave early, in order to enable his/her partner to take the remainder of the leave, must give his/her permission for us to release any information confirming his/her return to our employment and the period of adoption leave and pay to his/her partner's employer, before we may do so. Such information will not be disclosed otherwise, which may result in delay in the partner receiving any remaining adoption pay or his/her ASPL being authorised by his/her employer.

Paternity - statutory paternity leave (SPL)

Paternity legislation has changed significantly over recent years and new fathers now have much more protection than ever before. This has included the introduction of transferral of leave between parents. This could be an administrative challenge, so my advice is to keep it as basic and straightforward as possible, and don't be tempted to change or replace any of the guidelines below. Also note that same-sex partners have rights to paternity leave.

Subject to meeting the eligibility requirements, employees who are the father of a child or its mother's husband/partner, and who expect to have responsibility for the child's upbringing (or an adoptive parent who is not taking adoption leave) are entitled to two weeks' paid statutory paternity leave. Statutory paternity leave is paid at the same rate as lower rate SMP (or 90% of the employee's earnings, if this is less).

This entitlement applies to employees who:

- are the natural or adoptive father of a child born, or placed with them for adoption, or the mother's husband or partner

- have a minimum of 26 weeks' continuous service ending with the 15th week before the expected week of the child's birth (for adoption, a minimum of 26 weeks' continuous service extending into the 'matching week'. This is the week beginning on a Sunday and ending on a Saturday in which the employee is notified of having been matched with the child.

- can demonstrate that they have (or expect to have) responsibility for the child's upbringing or are married to (or the partner of) the child's mother

- have average earnings at least equal to the lower earnings limit for NI contributions.

Leave must be taken during the eight-week period beginning with the child's birth date (or placement with its new parents for adoption within the UK, or date of entry into the UK for overseas adoptions). It can be taken either as one single week's leave or two consecutive weeks' leave, but a week can start on any day, for example Tuesday - Monday.

In the case of adoption, where a child is adopted jointly, either of the adoptive parents may take the two-week period of statutory paternity leave. The partner of an individual who is adopting will also be able to qualify for statutory paternity leave and pay if he/she can demonstrate that he/she is to share responsibility for the child's upbringing.

The employee must notify us of the date on which he/she intends to take statutory paternity leave by the end of the 15th week before the mother's expected week of childbirth (EWC). For an employee who is adopting a child in the UK, notification must be within seven days of the date on which the adopter has been officially notified of having been matched with the child. An employee who is adopting a child from overseas should give written notice in three stages as follows:

1. Where the employee has 26 weeks' qualifying service, he/she should inform us within 28 days of receiving official notification of the date on which he/she received official notification of the placement and the date the child is expected to enter the UK. If the employee has less than 26 weeks' qualifying service, the notice should be given within 28 days of completing 26 weeks' service.

2. In all cases, the employee must give 28 days' notice of the actual date he/she wants the adoption leave to start. For adoptions from abroad, this cannot be before the child enters the UK. This date can be changed by giving at least 28 days' notice (or as soon as is reasonably practicable). We will write to confirm receipt of this notification within 28 days of receiving it.

3. The employee must tell us the date the child entered the UK within 28 days of the entry.

Once the start date of the leave has been notified, employees may amend this, but must provide us with 28 days' notice of the new start date.

Paternity - Additional Statutory Paternity Leave (ASPL)

In addition to the standard statutory paternity leave, parents may choose to transfer up to six months of maternity/adoption leave to the father or partner once the mother/primary adopter has returned to work. This is known as additional statutory paternity leave ("ASPL")

Paternity - ASPL – eligibility

Note the term 'father' in this context may be the biological father, the spouse of the mother, or a partner or a civil partner under a same sex relationship.

To be eligible for additional statutory paternity leave the employee must have been continuously employed with us for 26 weeks ending with the 15th week before the baby is due. In an adoption situation, where the adoption is from within the UK, the employee must have 26 weeks' continuous service ending with the week in which the child's adopter is notified of having been matched with the child. Where the adoption is from overseas, the employee must have 26 weeks' continuous service by the end of the week in which the official notification of approval for adoption was received or, where the employee has changed employer since the official notification was received, since his or her employment with us began.

In both maternity and adoption situations, the employee must remain in continuous employment with us until the week before the first week of the additional statutory paternity leave.

Paternity - ASPL - giving notice to take additional statutory paternity leave

A leave notice, a signed declaration from the employee and a signed declaration from the mother/adopter to prove his/her eligibility are required. This is most easily provided on HMRC form SC7.

The 'leave notice' is a written notice specifying the child's expected week of birth (for adoption, the date the employee was notified of having been matched with the child); the child's date of birth/adoption and the dates the employee has chosen as the start date and end date for the period of leave.

The 'employee's declaration' must state that he/she is either the biological father, husband, partner or civil partner of the child's mother (for adoption, that he/she is either married to or the partner or civil partner of the adopter, and that the child has been matched with him/her for adoption); that he/she is taking the leave to care for the child and has, or expects to have, the main responsibility (apart from any responsibility of the child's mother/adopter) for the upbringing of the child.

The 'mother's declaration' (adopter's declaration' for those adopting) must state the mother's/adopter's name and address; the date of his/her return to work; his/her national insurance number; that the employee is the child's father or is the mother's/adopter's spouse, partner or civil partner; that the employee has, or expects to have, the main responsibility (apart from any responsibility the mother/adopter has) for the upbringing of the child; that the employee is, to the mother's/adopter's knowledge, the only person exercising the right to take additional statutory paternity leave in respect of the child; and that he/she consents to the employer processing this data.

The employee must notify us if his/her circumstances change, in case this affects his/her eligibility.

We also request a copy of the child's birth certificate (for adopters, evidence in the form of documents issued by the adoption agency showing: the name and address of the adoption agency; the date that the employee was matched with the child; and the expected date of placement) and details of the name and address of the mother's (or adopter's) employer (or his/her business address if he/she is self-employed).

In most cases we will want to check with the mother's/ adopter's employer that she has returned to work and the details of her maternity/adoption leave and pay taken to date. Written authorisation will always be requested from the mother/adopter before we do this.

Paternity - ASPL - taking leave

It is important to note that ASPL can only be taken once the mother/adopter of the child has returned to work; so both parents cannot take maternity leave and ASPL at the same time.

In a birth situation, an employee who qualifies for additional statutory paternity leave can take between two and 26 weeks' additional leave in the period that begins 20 weeks after the child is born and ends one year after the birth. The child's mother's period of maternity leave must have come to an end.

In an adoption situation, an employee who qualifies for additional statutory paternity leave can take between two and 26 weeks' leave in the period that begins 20 weeks after the child's placement for adoption and ends one year after the placement. The employee's partner's statutory adoption leave must have come to an end.

If the child's mother, or the other adoptive parent, dies in the first year of the child's life, the additional statutory paternity leave can begin at any time after the death and last until the child's first birthday.

Additional statutory paternity leave must be taken as one continuous period, in multiples of complete weeks. The minimum period of leave is two consecutive weeks and the maximum is 26 consecutive weeks.

Paternity - ASPL - notice requirements

The employee must give us at least eight weeks' notice of his/her start and finish dates for the additional statutory paternity leave.

Paternity - ASPL - changing the dates

If the employee withdraws his/her request to take ASPL less than six weeks before the start date and it is not reasonably practicable for us to accommodate the requested change, the employee may be required to start the leave on the date specified and this will end no later than six weeks after the date on which withdrawal notice was given to us or the end date specified in the leave notice, whichever is the earlier.

Once the period of additional statutory paternity leave has begun, if the employee wishes to return to work earlier than planned, we may delay a return until no later than six weeks after the date on which the employee gave us withdrawal notice, or the end date specified in the leave notice, whichever is the earlier.

If the employee wishes to vary the dates of the leave before the leave period has begun, he/she should give us at least six weeks' written notice of the change; failure to do so may result in us postponing the employee's return so that we have six weeks' notice of return.

Paternity – ASPL – pay

If the child's mother, or the other parent in an adoption situation, ends his/her period of maternity or adoption leave before taking the maximum entitlement to 39 weeks' statutory maternity pay, statutory maternity allowance or statutory adoption pay, the employee taking additional statutory paternity leave is entitled to be paid for the remainder of the 39-week period, assuming that he or she has average earnings of at least the lower earnings limit for national insurance purposes. In effect, the couple are paid for 39 weeks between them.

Additional statutory paternity leave is paid at the statutory maternity pay rate, or 90% of the employee's earnings, if this is less than the statutory rate.

Paternity - ASPL - terms and conditions

After a period of statutory or additional statutory paternity leave, an employee has the right to return to the same job on the same terms and conditions of employment as if he/she had not been absent.

An employee who takes a period of parental leave after his/her statutory paternity leave has same right of return provided that the period of parental leave does not exceed four weeks.

Paternity - ASPL - 'KIT' days

An employee on ASPL is entitled to take up to ten "Keeping In Touch" days (as for those on maternity/adoption leave) and the current provisions on redundancy during maternity leave and the right to be offered any suitable available vacancy is extended to him/her.

Flexible working

Employees who wish to change their working pattern or hours on their return from maternity/adoption/paternity leave must apply to do so following the statutory procedure for making flexible working requests.

Where possible, we will aim to grant such requests, however this is subject to the overriding needs of the organisation.

Surrogate parents

Any employee having a child placed with him/her through surrogacy will not normally be eligible for Statutory Maternity or Adoption Leave (any maternity rights, as you may expect, fall to the birth mother).

However the employee will be eligible for unpaid parental leave once he/she has attained a parental order (for further details of parental leave, see our policy on parental leave and time off for dependants). Also, if the intended parent is the biological father of the surrogate child then he would be eligible for paternity leave (subject to meeting all other eligibility requirements set out above). Implementation, monitoring and review of this policy.

Related policies

We also have the following related policies:

- *Absence and Sickness Policy*

- *Annual Leave Policy*

- *Equal Opportunities Policy*

Implementation, monitoring and review of this policy/procedure

This policy will take effect from (date). (Named person) has overall responsibility for implementing and monitoring this policy, which will be reviewed on a regular basis following its implementation (at least annually) and additionally whenever necessary.

Any queries or comments about this policy should be addressed to (named person).

6: Equal Opportunity Policy

Having a robust Equal Opportunity Policy is one of the most likely to keep you away from tribunals. If you are genuinely committed to your Equal Opportunity Policy you will earn the respect, commitment, and loyalty of your staff. This is one you need to make sure you get right.

Your Company Name:

Referred to in this policy as "The Company"

Introduction

The Company is committed to becoming an equal opportunity employer and to ensuring that all employees, job applicants, customers/clients and other people with whom we deal are treated fairly and are not subjected to unfair or unlawful discrimination. This policy is not contractual, but aims to set out the way in which The Company aims to manage equal opportunity.

Scope of this policy

This policy applies to all employees, including those on part-time, apprentice, fixed-term and job-share contracts, as well as other workers and agency staff.

Aims of this policy

Our policy is designed to ensure that current and potential workers are offered the same opportunities regardless of a protected characteristic (sex, race, disability, sexual orientation, religion or belief, age, marital status or civil partnership, pregnancy/maternity, gender reassignment) or indeed any other characteristic unrelated to the performance of the job. We seek to ensure that no one suffers, either directly or indirectly, as a result of unlawful discrimination. This extends beyond the individual's own characteristics, to cover discrimination by association and by perception.

We recognise that an effective equal opportunity policy will help all employees to develop to their full potential, which is clearly in the best interests of both employees and our business. We aim to ensure that we not only observe the relevant legislation but also do whatever is necessary to provide genuine equality of opportunity.

We expect everyone who works for us to be treated and to treat others with respect. Our aim is to provide a working environment free from harassment, intimidation, or discrimination in any form that may affect the dignity of the individual.

We further recognise the benefits of employing individuals from a range of backgrounds, as this creates a workforce where creativity and valuing difference in others thrives. We value the wealth of experience within the community in which we operate and aspire to have a workforce that reflects this.

Legal considerations

> **It is worth including these legal considerations, as it shows you have considered the various areas of legislation that bind it together. Follow this with the other considerations the policy covers.**

The main legislation that covers equal opportunity and discrimination is the Equality Act 2010. In addition, the following should be taken into consideration:

- *the Rehabilitation of Offenders Act 1974*

- *the Protection from Harassment Act 1997*

- *the Human Rights Act 1998*

- *the Sex Discrimination (Gender Reassignment) Regulations 1999*

- *the Racial and Religious Hatred Act 2006*

- *any Codes of Practice issued by the Equality and Human Rights Commission*

- *plus any amendments to the above legislation.*

Discrimination may be direct or indirect, and can take different forms, for example:

- *treating any individual less favourably than others on grounds of a protected characteristic (sex, race, disability, sexual orientation, religion or belief, age, marital status or civil partnership, pregnancy/maternity or gender reassignment)*

- *expecting a person, solely on the grounds stated above, to comply with requirements that are different to the requirements for others, for any reason whatsoever*

- *imposing on an individual requirements that are in effect more onerous than they are on others. This would include applying a condition (which is not warranted by the requirements of the position) which makes it more difficult for members of a particular group to comply than others not of that group*

- *harassment i.e. unwanted conduct which has "the purpose, intentionally or unintentionally, of violating dignity, or which creates an intimidating, hostile, degrading, humiliating or offensive environment" for the individual*

- *victimisation – i.e. treating a person less favourably because he or she has committed a "protected act". "Protected acts" include previous legal proceedings brought against the employer or the perpetrator, or the giving of evidence at a disciplinary or grievance hearing or at tribunal, or making complaints about the perpetrator or the employer or their alleged discriminatory practices*

- *discrimination by association, i.e. someone is discriminated against because he/she associates with someone who possesses a protected characteristic*

- *discrimination by perception, i.e. discrimination on the grounds that the person is perceived as belonging to a particular group, e.g. sexual orientation, religion or belief, irrespective of whether or not this is correct*

- *any other act or omission of an act, which has the effect of disadvantaging one person against another, purely on the above grounds.*

On all occasions where those in control of employees are required to make judgements between them, for example disciplinary matters, selection for training, promotion, pay increases, awards etc it is essential that merit, experience, skills and temperament are considered as objectively as possible.

Responsibility for this policy

To show your commitment to this policy put the following section in detailing who is responsible for it. This outlines that even though one person has overall accountability, all staff have a part to play in ensuring that the policy is adhered to.

The overall responsibility for implementing and monitoring the effectiveness of this policy rests with the senior management of The Company.

Managers and supervisors have a crucial role to play in promoting equality of opportunity in their own areas of responsibility.

All employees, irrespective of their job or seniority, will be given guidance and instruction, through our induction and other training, as to their responsibility and role in promoting equality of opportunity and not discriminating unfairly or harassing colleagues or job applicants, nor encouraging others to do so or tolerating such behaviour. Disciplinary action, including dismissal, may be taken against any employee found guilty of unfair discrimination or harassment.

Recruitment and selection

Unlike the previous policies, this one needs to emphasise that it covers individuals from the time they decide to apply for a position with you. In fact, alleged discrimination during the recruitment process applies to a large number of complaints each year. The following section, if followed, shows that you treat everyone fairly and that you are an equal opportunities employer. It can also prove to be a good guide for managers during the recruitment process.

We aim, through written instruction, appropriate training and supervision, to ensure that all those who are responsible for recruitment and selection are familiar with this policy and ensure it is applied.

Selection will be conducted on an objective basis and will focus on the applicants' suitability for the job and their ability to fulfil the job requirements. Our interest is in the skills, abilities, qualifications, aptitude and the potential of individuals to do their jobs.

Person specifications will be reviewed to ensure that criteria are not applied which are discriminatory, either directly or indirectly, and that they do not impose any condition or requirement which cannot be justified by the demands of the post. Questions asked of candidates will relate to information that will help assess their ability to do the job. Questions about marriage plans or family intentions or any other issues which may give rise to suspicions of unlawful discrimination should not be asked. Selection tests will be specifically related to the job and measure an individual's actual, or inherent, ability to do or train for the job.

Job adverts should encourage applications from all types of candidates and should not be stereotyped.

All adverts will state: "The Company is an equal opportunity employer and values diversity". Reference to this policy will also be made on job and person descriptions.

When advertising a position which has traditionally been done by one sex, adverts should specify they are open to both sexes.

Training and development

As with recruitment, you need to be committed to ensuring that all your staff are considered equally and fairly with regards to their personal and professional development. Outlining how you enforce equal opportunities when consdiering training demonstrates this.

The Company recognises that equal opportunity responsibilities do not end at selection, and is committed to ensure that wherever possible all employees receive the widest possible range of development opportunities for advancement.

All employees will be encouraged to discuss their career prospects and training needs with their manager. Opportunities for promotion and training will be communicated and made available to everyone on a fair and equal basis.

The provision of training will be reviewed to ensure that part-time workers, shift or remote workers or those returning to work following a break are able to benefit from training.

No age limits apply for entry to training or development schemes - these are open to all employees.

Terms and conditions of employment

Often smaller businesses recruit friends and family and, because of this, they are often tempted to play favourites. Outlining your commitment to equal opportunities in relation to all of your employees' terms and conditions will not only keep you on the right side of the law, but will also provide your staff with security and a feeling of equality. This, in return. will foster commitment and loyalty.

We will ensure that all of our policies including compensation, benefits and any other relevant issues associated with terms and conditions of employment, are formulated and applied without regard to a protected characteristic (sex, race, disability, sexual orientation, religion or belief, age, marital status or civil partnership, pregnancy/maternity, gender reassignment) or indeed any other characteristic unrelated to the performance of the job.

These will be reviewed regularly to ensure there is no discrimination. Length of service as a qualifying criterion for benefits will not exceed five years unless clearly justifiable.

Grievances, disputes and disciplinary procedure

We have already covered disciplinary and grievance as separate polices but it is important to emphasise that all staff will be treated fairly and equally should they need to initiate one of these procedures. It's worth noting it in this policy document as well.

Employees who believe they have been discriminated against and have not been able to resolve this informally are advised to use our internal grievance procedure. An employee who brings a complaint of discrimination must not be less favourably treated.

Harassment or bullying will not be tolerated, and any individual who feels that he/she has been subjected to harassment or bullying should refer to our bullying and harassment policy.

Equally, anyone who witnesses incidents of harassment or bullying should report this to his/her manager or an appropriate senior member of staff.

When dealing with general disciplinary matters, care is to be taken that employees or workers who have, are perceived to have, or are associated with someone who has, a protected characteristic are not dismissed or disciplined for performance or behaviour which could be overlooked or condoned in other employees or workers

Retirement

There is no recognised retirement age. However, contractually, you may still impose a retirement age as long as the ruling applies to everyone.

We have no fixed retirement age and anyone who wishes to work beyond state pension age may choose to do so.

Positive action

It is worth mentioning positive action in your policy as this can also cause conflict in the workplace. This is particularly useful if you operate in a region with is represented by a higher ratio of ethnic or cultrural group(s) than the national average.

We also recognise that passive policies will not reverse the discrimination experienced by many groups of people. To this end, if certain groups are under-represented within our business we will actively seek to encourage applications from those groups.

The decision as to which applicant is offered a post (either recruitment or promotion) must be based entirely on the merit of the individual. However, where two candidates are equally qualified and suitable in all other respects, we may decide to offer the post to a candidate who is from a group that is under-represented in our workforce at that particular level.

HR policies and procedures

The following section shows the commitment to equal opportunities from an HR and administrative perspective.

Our HR policies and procedures will be reviewed regularly to improve, amend or adapt current practices to promote equality of opportunity within our business.

Communication of this policy

All job applicants, employees and workers will be made aware of this policy and a copy will be included in the Employee Handbook, given to all employees on joining us. Customers / clients may also be made aware of this policy.

In addition, employees will be reminded of the policy through such means as advertisements, application forms, posters, training courses and emails.

Related policies

We also have the following related policies:

- Equal Opportunities tend to cross over all areas of the business and therefore all other policies will be relative to this policy.

Implementation, monitoring and review of this policy

This policy will take effect from (date). (Named person) has overall responsibility for implementing and monitoring this policy, which will be reviewed on a regular basis following its implementation and may be changed from time to time.

Relevant data will be collected to support this policy. Personal details provided by employees or job applicants for the purposes of equal opportunity monitoring are confidential, will be kept apart from all other records and not used for any other purpose.

Any queries or comments about this policy should be addressed to (Named person).

7: Parental Leave & Time Off for Dependants Policy

On June 30th 2014 the Government brought in new legislation extending the right for everyone with more than 26 weeks sevice the ability to apply for flexible working. As of this date all employers will be obligated to consider all requests in a reasonable manner. However, employers still have the right to refuse the request providing they can justify their decision on business grounds. Once again, the importance of a good policy is paramount.

Your Company Name:

Referred to in this policy as "The Company"

Introduction

The following document sets out our policy on parental leave and time off for dependants. Any employee who has any questions about this policy or about any other aspects of parental leave or dependant care rights should contact their manager.

This policy is not contractual but sets out the way in which we plan to manage this.

Scope of this policy

This policy applies to all employees, including those on fixed-term contracts.

Aims of this policy

This policy aims to explain the statutory rights to parental leave and time off for dependants and the process that should be followed by employees who wish to take such leave.

Legal considerations

The following pieces of legislation apply to this policy:

- *The Employment Rights Act 1996*

- *The Maternity and Parental Leave etc. Regulations 1999 – The Parental Leave (EU Directive) Regulations 1999 – the Parental Leave (EU Directive) Regulations 2013.*

Definitions

Parental leave is time off work to look after a child or to make arrangements for the good of the child. A disabled child is one for whom the parents receive disability living allowance.

A dependant is a parent, spouse, civil partner, child or someone who lives with the employee as part of the family or who reasonably relies on the employee for care in the event of illness or injury.

Eligibility to take parental leave

Employees have the right to parental leave if they have one year's continuous employment AND

a) *are the parent of a child who is under five years old and are either named as a parent of the child on the birth certificate or have formal parental responsibility for the child although separated in marriage and/or not living with the child OR*

b) *have adopted a child who is under the age of 18. This entitlement lasts for five years from the date on which the child is placed for adoption or until the child's 18th birthday, whichever is the sooner OR*

c) *have acquired formal parental responsibility for a child who is under five years old OR*

d) *have a disabled child under the age of 18.*

e) *Note that foster parents are not entitled to parental leave.*

Taking parental leave

A maximum of 18 weeks' parental leave is available for each eligible child. Part-time employees are entitled to parental leave on a pro-rata basis.

Parental leave is unpaid.

Parental leave should be taken in blocks of one week. If taken in blocks of less than a week, a full week will be deducted from the employee's entitlement (unless the child is disabled, in which case leave may be taken in multiples of a day).

A maximum of four weeks' parental leave can be taken each year. Note: a year is calculated as a twelve-month period commencing at the anniversary of starting employment with us (if the employee already has a child under five) or commencing with the child's date of birth if the employee already has twelve months' service.

Parental leave must be taken within five years of the birth/formal adoption of the child, other than for parents of disabled children who may take the leave at any time up to the child's 18th birthday.

Upon returning from parental leave of four weeks or less employees are entitled to return to their same job, on the same terms and conditions. If the employee takes more than four weeks' parental leave (for example where leave spans across an anniversary of employment and the employee decides to take both years' entitlements, or leave is taken for more than one child) the employee is entitled to return to the same job unless this is not reasonably practicable, in which case he/she must return to a job which is suitable and appropriate. The right to return is on terms and conditions not less favourable.

Giving notice to take parental leave - planned parental leave

Employees must give at least 21 days' notice before a period of parental leave begins, of both the start and end dates of the leave period the employee wishes to take.

Parental leave may be postponed for up to six months due to the requirements of the business (except for prospective parents and adoptive parents for time off requested immediately after the time the child is born or is placed with the family for adoption.)

The reason for any such postponement will be explained, but if an employee feels that a request for leave has been unreasonably refused or postponed, he or she may raise a grievance using our grievance procedure.

Employees should provide their manager with a copy of the child's birth certificate or adoption certificate (only required for the first period of parental leave for each child).

Giving notice to take parental leave – unplanned parental leave

Employees who wish to take leave immediately after a baby is born or a child is placed with them for adoption, should give at least 21 days' written notice before the beginning of the week in which the birth or adoption is expected.

Once the timing of the leave is agreed, a copy of the child's birth certificate or adoption certificate should be provided to the employee's manager (only required for the first period of parental leave for each child and in the case of new born babies to be provided as soon as possible).

Time off for dependants

All employees have a right to take reasonable time off (unpaid) in the case of emergencies relating to a dependant. This right applies to all employees, irrespective of their length of service or hours worked.

The right to time off is as follows:

- *to help when a dependant is ill or injured*

- *to cope when the arrangements for caring for a dependant unexpectedly break down*

- *when a dependant gives birth*

- *when a dependant dies*

- *to deal with an unexpected incident involving a dependent child during school hours or on a school trip.*

Time off for dependants - taking leave

Employees may only exercise this right if they tell their manager about the reasons for time off. Where possible the manager should be notified beforehand, but if this is not possible, notification should be as soon as reasonably possible. Failure to notify us could lead to disciplinary action under our disciplinary procedure for absence without leave.

Note that there is no definition of "reasonable" and no legal limit on the duration of this leave, but as a guide, we would expect that the amount of leave will be one to two days in order to deal with the immediate problem and make any longer term arrangements.

This leave is not intended to be used for the purposes of caring for a sick dependant.

Terms and conditions of employment

During any parental leave or time off for dependants employees will remain bound by their duty of good faith to (name of company) and their duty not to disclose confidential information.

They remain employed during parental leave or time off for dependants and accrue unbroken continuity of service and also continue to accrue statutory holiday entitlement under the Working Time Regulations.

Parental leave and time off for dependants is unpaid.

Related policies

We also have the following related policies:

- *Maternity, Adoption and Paternity Leave*

Implementation, monitoring and review of this policy

This policy will take effect from July 2014. The (named person) has overall responsibility for implementing and monitoring this policy, which will be reviewed on a regular basis following its implementation (at least annually) and additionally when necessary. Any queries or comments about this policy should be addressed to the (named person).

Relevant Legislation

The following is a list of current legislation and guidelines affecting workplace and employee law. You don't need to read them all, but some awareness of the range of legislation may be of interest.

- *Agency Workers Regulations 2010*
- *The Automatic Enrolment (Offshore Employment) Order 2012*
- *Employment Agencies Act 1973*
- *Employment Rights Act 1996*
- *Employment Rights (Dispute Resolution) Act 1998*
- *The Employment Tribunals Act 1996 (Tribunal Composition) Order 2012*
- *The Employment Tribunals (Constitution and Rules of Procedure) (Amendment) Regulations 2012*
- *Equality Act 2010*
- *Fixed-Term Employees (Prevention of Less Favourable Treatment) Regulations 2002*
- *Health and Safety at Work Act 1974*
- *Human Rights Act 1998*
- *National Minimum Wage Act 1998*
- *Pensions Act 2004*
- *Protection from Harassment Act 1997*
- *Trade Union and Labour Relations (Consolidation) Act 1992*
- *Trade Union Reform and Employment Rights Act 1993*
- *The Transfer of Undertakings (Protection of Employment) Regulations 1996/2012*
- *Working Time Regulations 1998*

Further Advice and Support

Well that is it. Well done, you now have all the basic policies you need to legally comply and, more importantly, to help you operate efficiently and effectively. All of the above policies are included in *HR Basics for Small Business*, available to purchase from www.juliekellyhr.co.uk.

Books in this DIY HR series include:

Do It Yourself HR Basics for Small Business - Write Your Own HR Policies

Do It Yourself HR Basics for Small Business - Write Your Own Staff Handbook

Do It Yourself HR Basics for Small Business - Guide to Recruitment

Do It Yourself HR Basics for Small Business - Guide to Staff Contracts

HR Basics for Small Business is a one to one process where I can do all the work in writing your perfect HR polices, procedures and handbooks. While you have everything you need in these guides, it will still take you some time to put them all together. My service can also include updates throughout the year (as legislation and best practice changes). I'm also on hand to give you specific advice, guidance and support. You can consider me to be your own outsourced HR Department, without any employer's liabilities.

Useful Contacts

Chartered Institute of Personnel and Development (CIPD)
151 The Broadway, London, SW19 1JQ
www.cipd.co.uk
Phone 020 8612 6200
Fax 020 8612 6201

Department for Work and Pensions
www.dwp.gov.uk

Advisory, Conciliation and Arbitration Service (ACAS)
ACAS National (Head Office)
Euston Tower, 286 Euston Road,
London NW1 3JJ.
www.acas.org.uk
Customer services 08457 38 37 36.
Monday-Friday, 9am-5pm

CPSIA information can be obtained at www.ICGtesting.com
Printed in the USA
LVOW10s0248291014

410997LV00009B/82/P